D1579484

OBLIGATE
Carnivore

**Cats, Dogs & What it Really
Means to be Vegan
Revised and Expanded Second Edition**

JED GILLEN

Cover photo by Jerry Giles

ISBN: 1-4392-1120-5
ISBN-13: 9781439211205

Visit www.booksurge.com to order additional copies.

For Mona and Little Liv:
my two favorite girls of any species.

Preface to the Second Edition

In 2003, when *Obligate Carnivore: Cats, Dogs & What it Really Means to be Vegan* was first published, I lived in drizzly Seattle and was the owner of vegancats.com: the premier (if I do say so myself) online destination for vegan pet food. My days were spent in a damp, dark warehouse: selling, taping up cardboard boxes filled with, and answering endless questions about vegan cat and dog food. This issue occupied an unhealthy proportion of my time and consciousness at that point in my life; thus it seemed only natural to devote an entire book to it.

Since that time, many things have changed. It has been several years now since I retired from the vegan pet food business[1]; currently, I make my living as an independent filmmaker in sunny Los Angeles. Along with my partner, the beautiful vegan actress and model Mona Gillen, my days are now spent lying around the pool and occasionally pointing a

---

1 but fear not: vegancats.com is still alive and well, under the capable ownership of Ryan Wilson and Courtney Ernster of veganessentials.com

camera at something; the only time I ever have to think about vegan cat and dog food anymore is once in the morning and once at night when we feed our four cats (three vegan and one meat-eater; I will explain a bit later).

While all relevant material relating to the issue of vegan cats and dogs that appeared in the first edition is included here as well—along with some important updates—the astute reader may observe that this discussion does not pick up until about halfway through, and that the early portion of this edition is essentially all brand new material. This change in focus is partially attributable to the change in the focus of my own life. The primary criticism of the original edition was that some people felt it came off a little too sales pitch-y; well, I now have nothing to sell.

But there's more to it than just that.

I set out to write *Obligate Carnivore* with a very specific objective in mind: I wanted to show other vegans why I feel that feeding cats and dogs a meat-based diet is inconsistent with a vegan ethic. To do so effectively required that I not only address some of the common concerns that people have regarding feeding vegan food to their companions (taurine, anyone?), but also that I try to define very clearly what our objectives as vegans are in the first place.

Although the *"& what it really means to be vegan"* parts of the book were merely intended to lay some groundwork for the larger argument about cats and dogs, they unexpectedly struck a chord with a number of people for whom the book wasn't even intended—vegans without cats and dogs in their homes as well as whatever non-vegans happened to read it. I received no fewer than three emails from people who'd given a copy to their vet, only to have the vet decide to become vegan themselves! Again and again, I was urged to write a second book: one that expanded upon the *& what it really means to be vegan* theme, but without limiting myself so much in terms of my target audience.

I have never felt particularly inspired to write a book that tries to persuade non-vegans to become vegan, as there are already plenty of good books out there doing just that. John Robbins is always a compelling read, Matthew Scully's *Dominion* is a personal favorite, and if I were ever inclined to worry about these books' lack of edge and attitude, there's always *Skinny Bitch*—the book I like to think I might have written had nature seen fit to equip me with another X chromosome and better marketing instincts. However, the idea of writing a book on veganism for vegans—one that helps us to better understand ourselves, our relationship to the rest of the world, and how we can be a little bit more effective in achieving our objectives—has intrigued me.

For one reason or another, I never quite got around to writing such a book. Yet when the first printing of *Obligate Carnivore* recently ran out, it seemed to present a golden opportunity to fix it up a bit: to create, in the guise of a second edition, the better, more well-rounded book that you currently hold in your hands.

Jed Gillen
Los Angeles, CA
summer, 2008

"...& What it Really Means to be Vegan"

Hitler, Einstein & Weird Al Yankovic

"How do you deal with the fact," someone once asked me in an email, "that Hitler was a vegetarian?"

"The same way," I wrote back, "that you deal with the fact that Stalin ate meat." Ha ha! See what I did there? I can be pretty clever sometimes! If you don't like that one, here are a couple of other possible answers:

"You know what else Hitler did? He wore shoes. Do you wear shoes? You do? What are you, some kind of Nazi?" Or: "What's to deal with? I'm vegetarian for the same reason he was—because I hate the Jews."

All too often, however, vegans in this situation instead scramble to account for this perceived contradiction. They'll point out that he was only a vegetarian for part of his life, or argue that he was motivated solely by health—rather than ethical—concerns. This discomfort, I believe, stems from a subconscious belief that everyone in the world can be neatly located somewhere along a moral continuum. The worst people in history are the despots and serial killers

(Pol Pot, Jeffrey Dahmer...), while the very best and brightest our species has produced—you, me and Weird Al Yankovic, to name only a few—are vegans. As proof of our inherent superiority, we often circulate lists of the many brilliant people throughout history who are purported to have been in favor of animal rights: Leonardo da Vinci, Aristotle, and Albert Einstein prominently among them.

Now, I must confess to being somewhat unsure whether Einstein was actually a vegetarian or not. Many pro-animal statements have been attributed to him[2], but then again, the same is true of Darwin—and I happen to know on very good authority that for every five minutes he spent studying the eponymous tortoises during his famed visit to the Galapagos Islands, he spent at least another half hour cooking and eating them[3]. Just for the sake of the argument, though, let's assume that Einstein was, in fact, vegetarian. Hell, let's say he was vegan. Let's say that he went to the opening of the first McDonald's in 1940 and handed out fliers with a picture of a bloody cow head on them. Every time he went out to eat, Einstein, let's say, always interrogated the waitress to determine whether there were any tiny, hidden animal ingredients in anything he was considering ordering. All of that would constitute a real feather in our collective cap, right? I mean, they didn't call Einstein's theory of relativity "special" because it was retarded. Here we have a guy who was so smart that to this day his name is synonymous with the concept of intelligence—and he was one of us!

2 "It is my view that the vegetarian manner of living, by its purely physical effect on the human temperament, would most beneficially influence the lot of mankind." – Einstein

3 "The love for all living creatures is the most noble attribute of man. Wow, this is good tortoise. Can you pass the ketchup, FitzRoy?" – Darwin

Okay, but then how do we account for Niels Bohr?

Although the mean eighth-graders who sat in the back of your school bus may not have known it (Einstein and, of course, Poindexter—the geeky scientist from the Felix the Cat cartoons—sharing standard-bearing status for intelligence among mean eighth-graders), Niels Bohr was a Danish Nobel Prize-winning physicist from the early 20th century: a contemporary of Einstein who was held by mutual colleagues in similar esteem. He may not enjoy the same level of name recognition today, but that doesn't mean that Bohr was a complete moron. If you played Trivial Pursuit against him, he'd almost assuredly be in the winner's circle correctly identifying Steve McQueen as the star of *The Great Escape* before you'd even had a chance to touch the dice. And yet, somehow, while you, Jennie Garth and I managed to stumble upon an understanding of the ethical principles underlying veganism, Bohr blissfully spent his entire life eating Danish meatballs made out of pork and veal.

One common conspiracy theory that we hear floating around the animal rights community holds that the majority of people do not make the connection between meat and the animals from whence it is derived due to a concerted effort by the slaughter industry to flimflam consumers into believing that all of their products grow on a magical meat tree and do not involve animals at all. "Why else would they call it 'beef' and not 'cow'?" these conspiracy theorists might ask, "or 'ham' and 'pork' instead of 'pig'?"

Okay, "soylent green" I'll give you; but what about "chicken"? Just about the only time you ever hear the food that is made out of chicken not called "chicken" is when it's

called "buffalo wings" and that—biological absurdity aside—
is almost kind of even more viscerally disturbing. Fish, they
call "fish". Turkey, "turkey". "Lobster". "Monkey brains". I
could go on and on. "Cod liver oil" is, in fact, the oil from
the liver of a cod; nothing could be more straightforward
than that. And if you really want to get down to it, "beef",
"ham" and "pork" and all old Latin or French words that
mean "cow", "ass" and "pig", respectively—and by "ass" I do
not mean the animal. You want truth in advertising? How
about the fact that "ham", while not actually telling you what
kind of animal it comes from, specifically indicates what *part*
of the animal it is—*the ass?*

"Here," Hormel and whoever else sells those tinned
ham products that you see in the supermarket are very
overtly saying, "wouldn't you enjoy a can of smashed asses
this holiday season?"

More to the point, where this theory really flops is that
it attributes to relative idiots like you, me, and Christina
Applegate, a power of penetrating insight that eluded Niels
Bohr and, for that matter, Mozart, Doogie Howser and
countless other meat eating geniuses throughout history.
Seriously: you expect me to believe that the guy who came
up with the "Bohr model" of the atom couldn't see through
the clever subterfuge to figure out that "pork" is made out
of pigs... but the actress who played Kelly Bundy could??
That is insane!

Much to the contrary, a few years ago, a (vegan) friend
of mine did a correlative study comparing diet choice with
various demographic metrics and found the strongest
relationship of all was an *inverse* correlation between

veganism and level of education! Since I expect that a lot of vegans are reading this, I'll explain what this means in simpler terms: Jeopardy champions and people with doctorates? Most of them eat meat. Trailer park denizens and those holding degrees from community colleges? Vegans, all! While there are probably any number of ways we could plausibly rationalize away this conclusion, I have several reasons for preferring to let it stand:

First, it's hilariously ironic. Vegans and other progressives have a really bad habit of going around panning anyone whose viewpoints differ from our own as morons, and it just kind of strikes me as funny to reflect that, on average, we're actually less educated than everyone else.

Second, I believe that there are some contexts in which stupidity can actually be an asset. For example: what proportion of employee-of-the-month awards in fast food restaurants do you think are awarded to mentally-challenged people? *100%!* Because whereas everyone else screws around, ignores sanitary guidelines, and transmutes into Hamburger Claus whenever friends or pretty girls drop in, there's always that one Down's Syndrome guy who takes his job deadly seriously and ends up being a far more valuable worker; it's a tortoise/hare situation, essentially. Maybe if we embrace—rather than ignore—our relative lack of education, it'll motivate us and keep us from getting complacent.

Third and finally, think about it: is this result really all that shocking? How many vegan doctors, lawyers, rocket scientists, college presidents and the like do you know? And how many, on the other hand, that are in the employ of hipster coffee shops and record stores? For that matter, how many vegans are "uneducated" only to the extent that they're fourteen-year-old girls still in the ninth grade? Personally, when I first became vegetarian I found it entirely untroubling to believe that I was more intelligent than Niels Bohr because a) I was a teenager and therefore figured I was smarter than pretty much everyone else already, and b) I had just failed out of 11th grade Physics and had never even heard of the guy!

Satori

Those of you who are not vegetarian will be asked to forgive the arrogance of those of us who are if we tend to view our dietary transformation as an awakening of sorts—roughly akin to attaining spiritual enlightenment. I understand why that must be irritating. I hate when people presume to possess a superior knowledge or perspective about something and then deign to patronizingly instruct me about how I might yet mitigate my many shortcomings. Like the crazy Christians who proselytize on the street and shout "Jesus loves you!" at my back, even though I have just gruffly hurried past in a manner that was specifically intended to invite them to go fuck themselves—I mean, a) what god in his right mind would choose to reveal himself to, for example, those crackpots with the sandwich boards that say "God hates sinners!" on them and yet not to, say, Gandhi, and b) can't Jesus take "no" for an answer? It's pathetic after a while. It's almost like I'm back in junior high and Jesus keeps sticking notes in

my locker: I love you. Do you love me? with checkboxes for
yes or no. Take a hint, okay, Jesus? I only like you as a friend.
I think we should see other people.

In much in the same way that everyone is supposed to
be able to recall with photographic clarity exactly where
they were and what they were doing when Kennedy was
shot[4], when JFK Jr.'s plane went down[5], and when Princess
Died in that car crash[6], many vegans can pinpoint the exact
moment that they experienced their awakening. Many
describe it as being almost as if a switch was thrown in their
brains, and that's sure how it felt to me as well. When I
became vegetarian, I felt almost as if I were receiving a divine
dispensation—my own burning bush moment, if you will.

I was seventeen years old, sitting at the counter of a
New York deli, exactly one bite into a six-inch thick chicken
sandwich. Although I had previously had no particular incli-
nations regarding animal rights—in the preceding week, for
example, I had a) ordered a meat-lover's pizza at Pizza Hut,
b) eaten veal parmagiana, and c) worn a pair of skintight
black leather pants to school—as I bit into the not inexpen-
sive stack of bird flesh, it suddenly flashed through my brain
that chicken (the food) and chicken (the animal) weren't just
homonyms by random accident but because the two things
were actually one and the same. I found myself struggling
against peristalsis. Now of course it's not that I hadn't understood this on some level already—oranges are orange,

---

4 me: not born yet
5 I dunno. Eating a sandwich, maybe?
6 cleaning out the chicken barn at Farm Sanctuary, California, with a native Brit who was
so overcome with joy at the news that he literally fell over onto a bale of hay laughing

and chicken is made from chicken; what could be more clear?—but somehow, and I know that a lot of vegans can appreciate what I mean by this, it just hadn't *clicked* until that moment. I was horrified: *I was eating a dead animal!* With the exception of one time in college when the cafeteria lady lied to me about which burritos were the beef and which the bean[7], this was the last bite of meat I have ever taken.

Much of my exposure to Eastern thought has, regrettably, been through contact with pseudo-intellectual, Zen-koan-understanding pompous blowhards in coffee shops—the very same people who have forever turned me off to the music of Tom Waits, the books of William Faulkner, and the smell of clove cigarettes. Yet, despite this context and my general skepticism, the traditional Buddhist belief that the path to enlightenment requires learning to still your mind has always stood out to me as highly reasonable. It just seems intuitive that if you could get that constant every-day chatter of your thoughts to shut up for a minute, you would have the opportunity to reflect on whatever more meaningful knowledge, if any, you might have hidden in the deeper recesses of your brain. In light of this, I have always wondered if it might have been more than just a coincidence that it was immediately following an entire afternoon spent standing in line at the DMV—one of the most boring, mind-numbing activities in the history of humankind—that I experienced my chicken/chicken epiphany[8].

---

7 "Do these have bean or beef in them?" I asked. "Bean," she said. "Bea-na?" I clarified, enunciating carefully. "Not bee-fa?" "BEA-NAH!" she answered, annoyed. I took a big bite, and gagged. They were bee-fah

8 the word "epiphany", incidentally, is derived from the Greek epiphaneia, which means "manifestation". Initially, it referred to the aforementioned Jesus's manifesting himself as

It is really not my intention here to draw too tight of a parallel between the "enlightened" moral position of ethical vegans and the spiritual enlightenment of Buddhist monks because—I'll be honest with you—I'm not a Buddhist monk and therefore have no idea of what their particular form of enlightenment consists, assuming that it even exists at all. The couple of times that I've tried meditating, I couldn't get my thoughts to shut up for more than about a half second because every time they started to, my brain would immediately ruin everything by noticing and then having to brag about it ("There! See? My mind is entirely quiet. I'm the greatest meditator in the world!"). Nonetheless, I think it may be instructive to carry this analogy just a bit further:

A typical student of Zen who you might read about (assuming, of course, that you are a pretentious schmuck who studies Eastern philosophy) thinks that he's just out for a quiet walk in the forest, when *Wham!* His Master jumps out from behind a tree and clubs him in the back of the head with a fallen branch. "Son of a—!" the startled student cries out in pain, dropping, in a dramatic flutter of robes, to the ground at his Master's feet. Has he simply been knocked unconscious? Perhaps. Yet Buddhist tradition holds that, under certain circumstances, a blow to the head may also trigger a spontaneous understanding of whatever it is that

---

the messiah to the three wise men on January 6th, 0001. January 6th. So you know those nativity scenes that people put in their yards around Christmas each year? Those depict a scene that didn't occur until Jesus was already twelve days old. I mean, I understand that on Christmas eve itself there was no room at the inn and they found themselves in a tight spot, but... you'd think a room would've opened up within the next twelve days, wouldn't you?

enlightened Buddhists supposedly understand. The Japanese term *satori* is sometimes used to describe this instantaneous shift in consciousness.

So, one might plausibly inquire, does that mean that boxers, football players, and the wives of alcoholic rednecks have a higher rate of enlightenment than the rest of us? No; because getting hit in the head, by itself, isn't enough to bring about *satori*. Only those who are prepared to receive enlightenment are able to experience this transformation.

Activism, of course, takes many forms, but one of the most common is what could be called the "electroshock" method. I trust that most readers have viewed enough medical dramas on television to understand the metaphor: when the heart has stopped, a powerful jolt of electricity administered directly to the cardiac muscle can sometimes cause it to restart. I find this a fascinating medical procedure because, under normal circumstances, an electric shock delivered directly to the heart is likely to *stop* it. This is kind of like the paradox of radiation—which both causes and cures cancer[9]. The word "electroshock" strikes me as particularly apt not only because it relies on "shocking" images and statistics, but also because it carries with it the same grave risk of doing the exact opposite if unwisely applied.

"Kosher slaughter laws," a typical vegan activist might announce, upon discovering the sliver of a conversational opening, "require that the hearts be removed and shown to the animals so that they can watch themselves die" or

---

9 or, if you prefer, Homer Simpson's insightful description of alcohol: "the cause of—and solution to—all of life's problems"

"here—how'd you like to see a video of baby monkeys being scalded alive? It's part of an experiment, paid for by Republicans and corporate executives, to determine the optimal temperature of luxury yacht hot tubs". And when this approach fails to induce *satori*—as is almost invariably the case—we simply assemble more facts, statistics and gruesome photographs and keep clubbing away: an exercise in futility that only serves to marginalize our movement further and further, thus perhaps doing more harm than good.

One of the embarrassing truisms of the vegan movement is that almost all of us, despite our most earnest efforts, are surrounded by parents, siblings, co-workers, and friends who remain entirely resistant to our message—and who, in point of fact, are more likely than the average stranger to tease us mercilessly about it. If you are vegan and have a younger brother, for example, showing him all of the graphic slaughterhouse footage in the world is about 1% as likely to persuade him to become vegan himself as it is to induce him to chew up a piece of hamburger meat and then open up his mouth and show it to you before he swallows.

Under the vast majority of circumstances, to strike someone over the head with a tree branch is to commit a felony; enlightenment is induced in only those individuals whose minds are prepared to receive it. *Diet for a New America* is a great book, but not everyone who reads it finds it persuasive. If you read it and were inspired to make wholesale changes to your lifestyle, this does of course says something about the efficacy of the book—but it also says a lot about you. Vegans are not, as I have attempted to demonstrate, inherently any smarter (what about Bohr?) or more moral (what about Hitler?) than anyone else—yet there is clearly *something* that sets us apart.

I am one of those people who never goes to the doctor for fear of an unwelcome diagnosis, so I can certainly understand why the undertaking of such a self-examination may seem distasteful to many readers, and why most have probably never even considered the question before. However, it is my hope that after reading the next couple of chapters, you'll agree that the insight to be gained is sufficient to justify the inquiry.

Jabbing & Stomping

If there is ever a vegan on a sit-com, she—and it's *always* a she—is the ditzy whackjob who is invited to dinner and then ruins it for everybody else by humorlessly lecturing them on the arcana of the animal agriculture industry. The male lead—attracted to her because, despite her flaws, she's nonetheless kind of hot in a free-spirited, Michelle Phillips-ish sort of a way[10]—is initially so infatuated with her that he completely fails to notice how crazy she is. Before the half-hour's up, though, you can bet that he'll have dumped the zany bitch, and then—his lesson having been well learned—humorously offered to treat his friends to a round of ham-

---

10 for a while, Mona and I were supporting ourselves working as extras for TV, movies and commercials, during which time we got hired to portray all different types of people. Among other things, we have been a lawyer and her client on *Boston Legal*, guests of the Tipton Hotel on *The Suite Life of Zack and Cody*, and members of the famous Network that follows that "can you hear me now?" guy around. But one job that we were turned down for was: vegetarian restaurant patrons. Never mind the fact that, in real life, we ate in vegetarian restaurants all the time. Because I didn't have dreadlocks and she didn't have armpit hair, they didn't think we could pass for vegetarians

burgers.

I know some readers are probably inclined to write this off as an unfair stereotype cooked up by the networks in order to protect the financial interests of their corporate sponsors. Yet I'd have to argue that the stereotype would be a whole lot less unfair if progressives didn't blame so many things on corporate conspiracies. We vilify anyone who dares to run a successful business or vote Republican, blaming absolutely everything bad on them in the same way an earlier culture might have done with witches or evil spirits; no wonder everybody thinks our view of the world slightly nutty and off-kilter.

"Wardrobe! We need a black hat out here! And more mustache wax. Okay, places everyone! We're rolling in five... four... three... two and... action! Now you're walking down the sidewalk, and here comes a starving child begging for a penny to buy some bread... and you're pushing him to the ground and jabbing him in the eye with your umbrella! And now stomp on him! We're jabbing... we're stomping... jabbing... stomping... okay, now he's dead and we're moving along. Now you are stopping and looking in your black bag at the millions of dollars that you made exploiting honest working class folks with your crooked railroad enterprise... you're laughing evilly... and now you're taking the tips of your mustache between your fingers and twirling... we're laughing, we're twirling... laughing and twirling... twirling, *laughing, TWIRLING*... and

now here comes another starving child and we're jabbing and stomping again…"

That is my rendition of the progressive community
directing a silent film about a Republican CEO.

* * *

"You teach a child to read, and he or her will be
able to pass a literacy test."
- George W. Bush

Looking back, I can't help being slightly embarrassing
that the first two chances I had to vote in a Presidential
election, I darkened the oval for Bill Clinton both times. Not
to be overly judgmental, but the guy's twin legacies are com-
mitting perjury and chubby-chasing—not exactly the kind
of stuff that gets you a monument in the National Mall. On
the other hand, give him credit for being able to construct a
coherent sentence.

Bush again: "People say, how can I help on this
war against terror? How can I fight evil? You can
do so by mentoring a child; by going into a shut-in's
house and say I love you."

Err… how about if I just organize a scrap metal drive?
Look, it's not that I can't understand how a reasonably
intelligent person could say incredibly dumb things from
time to time. I personally get drunk and do just that approxi-

mately one to seven times per week. But, then again, I'm not the President. At worst, my idiocy threatens the wellbeing of some unlucky houseplants; there's little to no risk of it bringing an end to all advanced life on earth. More to the point, whereas I just make stuff up as I go along, the President's errors require the collaborative efforts of an entire staff of researchers, advisors, fact-checkers and the like. "Presidential speechwriter" would, I imagine, look pretty good on a resume if the President in question were a native English speaker like Bill Clinton; yet to confess that you had a hand in that whole bursting-into-the-homes-of-shut-ins-and-professing-your-love-for-them thing is no more than a half-step above admitting that you were head joke-writer for *Saved by the Bell: the College Years*.

Nonetheless, when Bush speechwriter Matthew Scully came out with his animal-rights-themed book *Dominion* a number of years ago, I was pretty excited about it. Albeit the size of a cinderblock and a little bit churchier than I generally prefer, *Dominion* remains one of my favorite animal rights books of all time. Scully's approach is a unique one: instead of trying to sell people on the merits of a radical, vegan lifestyle, he methodically demonstrates how well an animal ethic fits into a *conservative* worldview. The value of such an approach struck me as immediately self-evident.

I recall once being part of a discussion about how to reach out to more minorities with an animal rights message:

"We need to go into their communities and explain to them that an animal ethic is a traditional part of their culture," someone suggested. This, of course, was a terrible idea for two reasons: a) it is incredibly patronizing to go into someone else's community and explain to them the finer details of their own culture, and b) the step of ascertaining whether an animal ethic *actually was* a tradition for the minority group under discussion had been conspicuously skipped; thus the endeavor struck me as just a bit disingenuous. Matthew Scully, on the other hand, was not just some pandering radical trying to manipulate people, but a legitimate, card-carrying conservative with friends in the very highest of places. A whole segment of the population that would never dream of reading a book by, for example, a dirty hippie like John Robbins might be much more inclined to take his views seriously.

Given the potential impact of Scully's work, I was disappointed, when his book tour came through town[11], to see how many vegan activists chose not to attend his talk—boasting that they had no interest in anything a Republican had to say about anything—or, even worse, attended the talk and then sat in the back making rude, disruptive comments like seventh graders do when they have a substitute teacher. I was surprised that so many people reacted to Scully not as an ally, taking the message to a whole group of people that we have little ability to reach, but with a kind of hostility—as if his plan was to invade our movement and somehow make it impure. Caring more, it seems, about maintaining the

---

11   side note: Scully spoke at an excellent vegan restaurant called Café Ambrosia, where I was also asked to speak a few months later on behalf of Earthsave. Literally within days of my talk, Café Ambrosia was out of business and the local Earthsave chapter had folded. Coincidence?

homogeneity of the animal rights movement than they did about getting our message spread far and wide, they chose to shun rather than embrace Matthew Scully. The phrase I heard several times, muttered, at least metaphorically, with an ugly scowl: "There's no room in the animal rights movement for a Republican."

It was probably quite naive of me not to have seen this coming. There are people who claim that there is "no room" for drinkers and drug-users, "no room" for people who advocate direct action and property destruction, "no room" for people who *aren't* in favor of direct action, "no room" for Pamela Anderson[12]... in fact, I will be disappointed if this book doesn't prompt at least one idiot to declare that there's "no room" for me!

Okay, so maybe, just maybe, I'm interpreting this too literally. But come on—there's no room? *No room?* Have you been to an animal rights event where you had to turn people away at the door because your venue couldn't accommodate them all? Have you ever, even once, put together a demo where you outnumbered the police? Do you often find yourself refusing volunteers because there just isn't enough work for them to do? The vegan movement is still so tiny and insignificant that there are whole regions of the country in which no one even knows how to pronounce the

---

12 "Pamela Anderson, just being alive," a vegan girl of my acquaintance once opined at an animal rights meeting, "is an affront to women everywhere. I don't care how much she does for animals; she could never make up for the harm she does just by being herself. If she showed up here and wanted to volunteer to collect signatures for us, I would turn her away. Okay, well maybe if she put a bag over her head..." Malicious laughter of approval filled the room. If forced to translate into English, I would describe it as "yeah—fuck Pamela fucking Anderson!"

word ("Are you one of them [pauses to spit tobacco juice] VAY-Gins?")—I really don't think we're in any position to be picky about who we let in.

More to the point, doesn't the animal rights movement—insofar as it is, by definition, a movement that is supposed to be dedicated to protecting the rights of animals—have some moral responsibility to be at least moderately results-oriented when it comes to bringing about positive changes for animals? If Pamela Anderson standing outside the supermarket *without* a bag over her head would be able to collect more signatures than Pamela Anderson *with* a bag over her head, then aren't we kind of obligated to prefer the former?

Look, say what you will about Ms. Anderson's talents as an actress, the low production values of her home videos, or the fact that she chose to name her two sons—Brandon and Dylan—after the guys from *Beverly Hills 90210*, but to eschew her services as an activist because of her physical appearance strikes me both incredibly hypocritical and coun terproductive[13]. Like it or not, Pamela Anderson is the possessor of one of the world's most valuable piece of billboard real estate and she often chooses to stretch a PETA t-shirt over it—in my book, at least, that makes her awesome!

It is incredibly ironic that the progressive community—the very people who preach "tolerance" and "diversity"—are so often guilty of intolerance ourselves, that the

---

13 seriously: imagine putting Pamela Anderson, *without* a bag over her head, out on the street with a clipboard to gather signatures for a petition decreeing that all petition-signers shall be kicked twice weekly in the testicles by Italian soccer legend Roberto Baggio—how long do you think it would take for her to get a million signatures?

"diversity" we profess to value so often seems to apply only to those who meet our own very strict set of standards. "I was sitting next to this *Republican* on the bus today…" we tell each other, rolling our eyes with the full expectation that our meaning will be understood: that sharing a seat with any of the fifty million or so registered Republicans in the United States is roughly akin to sitting next to a stinking pile of dog crap.

Not everyone, of course, who is a vegan or otherwise involved in progressive activism is like this, but those of us who are—unfortunately—often seem to be those with the loudest mouths, who end up reflecting poorly on the rest of us.

It is my belief that a very small minority of people are attracted to progressive activism for the identical reason that one might become an ironic hipster douchebag[14], while the rest of us share a much more benign psychological makeup.

Let's talk about the douchebags first, shall we?

---

14 Ironic Hipster Douchebag (n): one who, when playing baseball, strikes out and then desperately tries to convince you that they did it on purpose in adherence to an ironic set of alternate rules in which the lower score wins. When an ironic hipster douche-bag walks down the street in a pair of Chuck Taylors and a thrift store mechanic's shirt with a nametag that says "Dick" on it, they are desperately hoping that passersby will think: "there goes a unique, interesting, iconoclastic individual". Whereas what passersby actually think is: "douchebag!"

The Unabomber

Every once in a while, the world produces an individual who seems to arrive on the scene at exactly the right moment, possessing the exact right set of ideas necessary to make an immediate and lasting impact. Freud at the turn of the twentieth century—*bang!* Everyone wants to sleep with their opposite sex parent, kill their same sex parent, and every thought, action and dream is the manifestation of subconscious motivations so pornographic that they'd make Jenna Jameson blush—great! Worrying excessively over minor details is somehow psychologically equivalent to retaining material in one's anus—sure, I guess that makes sense! For whatever reason, this was exactly the kind of stuff that the world was dying to hear as the Victorian age drew to a close.

More often, however, great thinkers produce ideas that are ahead of their time—or which are of the right time, but of the wrong planet—and which therefore may be scorned or ignored by their contemporaries, failing to illicit the desired *bang* in their lifetimes. Occasionally a frustrated, mentally unstable genius may lack the patience and confidence to contentedly assume that his vindication will be awarded posthumously, and will resort to using a cocktail of potassium sulfate, potassium chloride, ammonium nitrate and aluminum powder to create his own *bang*.

Ted Kaczynski—the "Unabomber"—is just such a person. A Harvard graduate and former professor at Berkeley, Mr. Kaczynski suffered a broken brain sometime in the late 1970's, whereupon he retired to an outhouse-sized shack in Montana and spent the next eighteen years hunting rabbits, growing vegetables, and letter bombing people who worked with computers and other forms of technology. Finally, in 1996, he sent a letter to the *New York Times*, promising to end his reign of terror if his anti-technological manifesto (*Industrial Society and Its Future*) were run in its complete form in a reputable publication. The *Times* initially balked, whereupon Bob Guccione stepped forward and offered to run it in *Penthouse* instead.

"I said 'reputable'," quipped the Unabomber[15].

There are several things wrong with Mr. Kaczynski's style of literary self-promotion, not the least of which is the fact that it required numerous innocent people to lose fingers and/or eyes and/or their lives. Had he simply hired an agent and gone on a book tour like everybody else, all of these people could have been spared a lot of agony and inconvenience. Sure, his method probably put his ideas in front of millions of additional readers than he wouldn't otherwise

15 boo-yah! Murderous hermit 1, porn magnate 0

have reached, but at the expense of announcing to the world that he's completely fucking nuts. Certainly there are other, more positive, ways that other authors have found to attract large audiences as well. Take J.K. Rowling as an example; to my knowledge she has never blown one single person's hand off. So perhaps, for instance, Kaczynski could have instead considered adding a boy wizard to his manifesto.

Furthermore, I find it absolutely impossible to condone Mr. Kaczynski's crazy, mad bomber haircut; I mean, I realize that you're anti-technology and everything, but for God's sake, even the Amish use scissors and a comb. Rule number one when the FBI is pouring all of its resources into trying to determine the identity of the mad bomber who is terrorizing the nation—and you are that mad bomber—is to get yourself down to the barbershop and tell them to make you look like an investment banker. I'm not even a mad bomber and I know this; it's just common sense.

Finally, I must confess to being largely unimpressed with the bulk of Kaczynski's manifesto, which promotes a brand of neo-Luddism that—unique method by which he brought it to the world's attention aside—is essentially no different than the kind of nonsense that you'd expect from any other Berkeley professor. The Unabomber's brilliance, in my opinion, lies in one fact and one fact alone: his decision to preface an agenda that could scarcely be more radical— he advocates tearing down modern society through violence and revolution—not only by attacking conservatives (i.e., those who want to "conserve" the status quo), but by slamming liberals as well.

I will offer a few choice quotes:

"Feelings of inferiority are characteristic of modern leftism as a whole... By 'feelings of inferiority' we [I believe that by "we", Kaczynski means himself and his imaginary friend] mean not only inferiority feelings in the strictest sense but a whole spectrum of related traits: low self-esteem, feelings of powerlessness, depressive tendencies, defeatism, guilt, self-hatred, etc. We [the imaginary friend is an invisible horse] argue that modern leftists tend to have such feelings (possibly more or less repressed) and that these feelings are decisive in determining the direction of modern leftism.

"Many leftists have an intense identification with the problems of groups that have an image of being weak (women), defeated (American Indians), repellent (homosexuals), or otherwise inferior. The leftists themselves feel that these groups are inferior. They would never admit it to themselves that they have such feelings, but it is precisely because they do see these groups as inferior that they identify with their problems. (We [the invisible horse lives underneath the ocean] do not suggest that women, Indians, etc., ARE inferior; we [he can't breathe underwater but, like a whale, can hold his breath for many hours] are only making a point about leftist psychology).

"Leftists tend to hate anything that has an image of being strong, good and successful. They hate

America, they hate Western civilization, they hate white males, they hate rationality. The reasons that leftists give for hating the West, etc. clearly do not correspond with their real motives. They SAY they hate the West because it is warlike, imperialistic, sexist, ethnocentric and so forth, but where these same faults appear in socialist countries or in primitive cultures, the leftist finds excuses for them, or at best he GRUDGINGLY admits that they exist; whereas he ENTHUSIASTICALLY points out (and often greatly exaggerates) these faults where they appear in Western civilization. Thus it is clear that these faults are not the leftist's real motive for hating America and the West. He hates America and the West because they are strong and successful.

"Words like 'self-confidence,' 'self-reliance,' 'initiative,' 'enterprise,' 'optimism,' etc. play little role in the liberal and leftist vocabulary. The leftist is anti-individualistic, pro-collectivist. He wants society to solve everyone's needs for them, take care of them. He is not the sort of person who has an inner sense of confidence in his own ability to solve his own problems and satisfy his own needs. The leftist is antagonistic to the concept of competition because, deep inside, he feels like a loser.

At first glance, Kaczynski's decision to unleash such vitriol might seem like manifesto suicide. After all, if your goal is to inspire people to blow up technology and disrupt the current power structure of the United States, who better to court than leftist radicals? When Manson sought willing executioners to carry out his murderous, messianic fantasies, whom did he recruit? *Hippie chicks!* No one loves a politically motivated bombing like a radical leftist and, Harvard degree hanging on the wall of his 10 x 12 shack, Kaczynski was smart enough to know this. So why go out of his way to alienate the very group of people to whom his message would most likely appeal? The answer is sanity itself: because he was trying to create a mainstream movement and saw no utility in cozying up to a group of people who would only muck it up and make it unwelcoming for everyone else.

Chew this one up thoroughly so that you can be sure to fully digest it: *the Unabomber*—the guy who, from a little cabin out in the middle of nowhere, mailed exploding packages to random people in an attempt to provoke a bloody revolution that would ultimately result in human beings voluntarily giving up all of their technological progress and returning to the stone age—meticulously distanced himself from the wacko douchebags of the far left because he knew that if they got involved, no one else would!

* * *

A prominent animal rights advocate and author, who I shall respectfully leave nameless, made the mistake a number of years ago of referring to both a young, blonde TV actress and a recent Miss Universe as "the new shape of the movement" during his speech at an animal rights conference. His point, as I understand it, was to make everybody feel good about the animal rights movement by equating its "shape" with the objectively shapely "shape" of these two empirically healthy, physically fit young women, as well as to inject a little levity into an evening of tedious speechifying with a harmless witticism. In the real world, the audience's choice would be to laugh or not laugh depending on how funny they personally found his pun to be; yet in the special, cannibalistic world of progressive activists, a group of self-appointed moral vigilantes took it upon themselves to beer-hall-putsch their way onto the stage and seize the microphone, publicly castigating and embarrassing a man who had done more for the cause of animal rights than perhaps three-quarters of the people in the room put together. Rape statistics were recited, suggesting a moral equivalency between sexual assault and publicly acknowledging the attractiveness of women whose careers are, at least in part, dependent upon that very attractiveness.

Although I was at that conference, due to a pressing prior engagement[16] it was not possible for me to be in attendance that night. When I returned to the hotel the next morning, I was filled in on the happenings of the previous night by various acquaintances—all of whom shared my sense of outrage at what had taken place.

To me, the three most offensive elements, in order from least to greatest, of this incident are as follows:

3) The joke itself, but only because it's sort of a reach.

---

16 i.e., bar-hopping with my old college roommate, Jon

2) The reinforcement these idiots gave to the all-too-true stereotype of leftists dealing with things by hysterically shouting down the opposing side instead of engaging them in intelligent discourse. One can only imagine the reaction of newcomers attending the conference in hopes of finding a supportive community of like-minded individuals. How fast would you run for the door upon instead discovering a group of people who, in response to a minor—perhaps imaginary—infraction, publicly bite the heads off of their most revered members? And, finally:

1) The fact that, although literally everyone I spoke to the next day was far more horrified by the behavior of the people who had jumped on stage than they were at the comment itself, the consensus was to remain silent and hope that the whole thing would just blow over.

As the Unabomber noted as well ("We emphasize that the foregoing does not pretend to be an accurate description of everyone who might be considered a leftist. It is only a rough indication of a general tendency of leftism"), the vast majority of vegans aren't douchebags. Most of us didn't join the movement because we never got over being picked last for kickball or similar psychological dysfunctions.

We just have a stupid tendency to allow those who did to speak for the rest of us.

I once set up an anonymous poll on a website I used to own asking vegans what they really thought about honey. The various choices were something along the lines of: a) I strenuously oppose it on ethical grounds; b) I'm not too worried about it personally, but generally avoid it out of respect for other vegans who are; c) I find it morally neutral and take no steps to avoid it; and d) I am eating from a jar of honey with a spoon as I type this with my other hand. Now of course I should probably have known better than to include a stupid joke answer like d) because, predictably, it was far and away the winner. Among people who took the question seriously, though, b) outpolled a) by a margin of approximately 10 to 1. In other words, the vast majority of vegans avoid honey for no better reason than to shelter themselves from judgment by the "vegan police": those who—operating on the premise that following a 99.5% vegan lifestyle is morally equivalent to child molestation—have taken it upon themselves to patrol the movement, rooting out and humiliating anyone who violates (or bends, or dares to have a different interpretation of) any of the rules.

In the original edition of *Obligate Carnivore*, I spoke of how, as owner of vegancats.com, I had once been boycotted for selling a homeopathic flea remedy that contained a small amount of "flea extract":

> "There is a certain 'vegan police' element here that allows such a big deal to be made out of what is clearly one of those gray-area issues (not all vegans consider fleas to be capable of having personal interests, and it is difficult to overlook the antagonistic relationship that naturally exists between a host and its ectoparasites), and I found it a little bit disturbing to find that certain members of our movement have apparently lost the ability for normal human com-

munication not involving angry words and threats of economic punishment (if this is how we treat *each other*, it's no wonder so many people have a bad image of us). But the biggest problem was the perplexingly illogical conclusion:"

These boycotters were willing to pull their financial support from a company that was, at worst, 99 44/100ths vegan and give it instead to… who? Petsmart? A company that makes literally millions of dollars annually selling food made from carcasses of tortured and murdered animals?

If a non-vegan celebrity does something remotely animal friendly—announces that they won't pose for photos wearing fur, adopts a dog from a shelter instead of a breeder, etc.—we generally treat them as though they've just developed a cure for cancer while simultaneously brokering a peace agreement between Israel and Palestine. Yet once someone has declared themselves to be a Vegan™, they suddenly find themselves held to a ridiculous standard.

A self-proclaimed vegan no longer receives any credit for anything positive they do—it is expected of a vegan to do positive things. But if they display inconsistency or imperfection of any kind, they are swiftly reduced to chum (no offense) in the vegan shark tank.

When we the ask the question "is such and such an item 'vegan'?", we ought to be reflecting upon how animals are affected by its proposed use, whereas our movement's witch hunt culture usually has us asking a slightly different question instead:"if I eat/buy/use this, will my status as a vegan be affected?" Thinking of things in such a distorted way has two negative consequences: we look like fringe lunatics when we worry excessively over insignificant things like mono and diglycerides—things which any reasonable person can see makes little or no difference to animals—and, as in the case of what we feed to our cats and dogs, we sometimes overlook areas in which we actually do contribute significantly to animal suffering on the grounds that the "vegan police" don't understand veganism well enough to bust us for it.

If veganism appears to outsiders as a kind of cult, it is because we tend to adhere to a predetermined orthodoxy about what we can and cannot do instead of applying our own common sense and making decisions for good, solid reasons.

Most people describe themselves as "animal lovers", but they have no interest in joining what appears to them to be the bizarre religion of animal rights. They prefer not to make their lives any more difficult than necessary, and get absolutely no psychological reward from being seen as radicals, revolutionaries or freaks. On the contrary, such labels are generally seen as an embarrassment—something to be actively avoided.

And that, my friends, is the primary reason why we're vegan and they're not.

Good Morning, Mr. Bullshit!

"As Gregor Samsa awoke one morning from uneasy dreams he found himself transformed in his bed into a gigantic insect."

So begins Kafka's famous story *Metamorphosis*, in which one of the characters spontaneously turns into a dung beetle as a metaphor for the drudgery and pointlessness of the average person's life. If you think about it, it's a nearly flawless analogy: not only is Kafka likening people to insects in general—animals that are widely believed to be driven more by robotic instinct than by rational thought[17]—but to that one specific arthropod whose life is so inextricably tied up with dung that they named it after it. And it's not just any old dung either, but usually—since the rise of modern

---

17 don't get all "vegan" on me here, okay? I don't know what drives insects; I am merely stating what is widely believed to be true about them.

agriculture, at least—that of cows: *the substance that is colloquially known as "bullshit".*

How perfect is that?

Five days a week, eight hours a day, dung beetles can be found hard at work at their bullshit jobs: making bullshit, selling bullshit, or simply moving bullshit from one place to another. In the evenings, they are so exhausted that they generally just come home and watch bullshit on TV for a few hours before falling asleep. On weekends, they entertain themselves with bullshit pastimes like fishing and golf; three lousy weeks per year are set aside for bullshit family vacations. At first the typical dung beetle may tell him or herself that such a routine is just temporary ("until my acting career takes off" or "while I work on my screenplay", e.g.), yet it is nearly inevitable that, within just a few short years, his or her hopes, dreams and *joie de vivre* will have become inextricably buried beneath a mound of cow leavings. The dung beetle settles down with the first moderately acceptable person to smile in his or her general direction on the commuter train, and raises a brood of grubs. Forty more years of drudgery purchases an RV, a condo in Florida and, ultimately, a nice slab of granite under which to lie.

Now I'm no literary critic but, if you ask me, the only real error in Kafka's *Metamorphosis* is the fact that no process of metamorphosis actually takes place in it. The very first time that we meet Gregor, he's just woken up to discover that he's been magically transformed into an enormous bug— so a more appropriate title might have been *Bang! You're a Dung Beetle* or *Good Morning, Mr. Bullshit!* More to the point,

Gregor's presto change-o transmutation is from figurative dung beetle to actual dung beetle, which seems to be more of a lateral shift than anything.

Metamorphosis, as anyone who is minimally acquainted with the life cycle of insects is already aware, is the process by which a *larva* becomes an *adult* having passed through the *pupa* state as an intermediate step. The closest human analogue of the pupal stage—a period of dormancy of variable length—is obviously the time that one spends as a pupil in college, living in a dorm. One enters college as a virtual child, bursting with energy, ideals, and optimism, only to emerge—just four to ten years later—as a full-fledged dung beetle: ready to go off to work, make some babies, and start paying off a mortgage.

I am embarrassed now—as I suspect many of us are—to contrast how much I thought I knew in my larval, teenage state (everything) with how much I actually knew (my locker combination, a whole bunch of Led Zeppelin lyrics). On the other hand, I am convinced that the idealism and rebelliousness that accompanies that stage of life had a lot to do with my becoming vegetarian.

If I know my human prehistory, it was somewhere around 2.2 million years ago that the first member of the genus *Homo* was born, and its name was *habilis*. *Homo habilis* is Latin for "handy man" and *H. habilis* was handy indeed, making tools out of stone and whatnot. A couple hundred thousand years later, *Homo erectuses* started popping up. *Homo erectus*, it goes without saying, is the all-time gayest species name ever. This was about the time that humans started dressing better and began to fancy themselves connoisseurs of cave art. Finally, about 300,000 years ago, *Homo sapiens* arrived on the scene. Thus, it has been about 30,000 decades since any major changes have occurred in the human lineage. Thirty thousand consecutive waves of children have hit puberty, only to discover—much to their horror—that the elder generation's lives, values, and belief systems are essentially based on bullshit.

> "Stop the oxcart at the olive tree around the corner," blushing teenagers in ancient Greece probably used to plead, humiliated at the thought of being seen in public with their parents. "I'll walk to the agora."
>
> "Bang log on rock two time then bang rock on rock one time so lame," we might imagine a prehistoric cave-teenager commenting about the hopelessly outdated musical preferences of the elder generation.

It's kind of ironic that all teenagers do the exact same things insofar as one of the things teenagers throughout history have in common is the unshakable belief that their generation is the first ever to feel the way they do.

Do you remember the movie *Dead Poets Society?* Very briefly, the plot runs something like this: a group of boys are attending some hoity-toity prep school in the late 1950's. Neil ("the sensitive, artistic one") has domineering, unloving parents who are intent on his becoming a doctor regardless of his own wishes. Knox ("the sex-crazed one") also has domineering, unloving parents who want him to become a doctor or something. Meeks ("the one whose geeky awkwardness spills onomatopoeically into his last name"), Todd ("the one who is played by Ethan Hawke"), Charlie ("one of the other guys in the movie")... yeah, pretty much all of them, as far as I can recall, have unloving parents who are forcing them to follow paths in life that are not of their own choosing.

Enter Robin Williams[18] in the role of John Keating, the poetry teacher who encourages the domineered, unloved students to follow their own dreams and to explore all of the beauty that exists in the world. A rogue lunatic, Keating demands that they rip pages from their textbooks, stand up on top of their desks during class, kick soccer balls after reciting a line of poetry, and all kinds of other crazy Zen master nonsense. His mantra, *carpe diem* (*"seize the day"*), stands in stark contrast to the kind of advice the students are accustomed to hearing from their parents and other authority figures ("wear sweater vests", "don't sneak out in the middle of the night to read poetry in caves with your friends", "never seize the day", etc.). While right at first they don't know what the hell to make of him, they eventually warm up to his poignant wackiness. Before long, they're sneaking out in the middle of the night to read poetry in caves with their friends and/or

---

18 brilliantly captured at the height of his wacky-yet-poignant *Good Morning, Vietnam* stage—that brief period of quality acting sandwiched in between his wacky-and-incredibly-annoying *Mork and Mindy* stage and his so-poignant-you-feel-like-punching-him *Patch Adams* stage

acting in plays and/or chasing girls all over town. They are *carpe-ing the diem.* They are *living.*

They are *finding it impossible to reconcile their newfound bohemian worldview with their parents' continued domineering behavior.* They are *spewing pathos onto movie audiences as if with a fire hose.* They are *engaging in gut-wrenching displays of teen angst the likes of which have not been seen since James Dean's "YOU'RE TEARING ME APART!!!"*

Strangely enough, at the exact moment that *Dead Poets Society* was released to theaters, I was a high school junior enrolled in a poetry class taught by a guy named Bob Adam who was, for all intents and purposes, Mary-Kate to John Keating's Ashley. Although Mr. Adam never said anything about animal rights—and was most likely a meat-eater himself—it was heavily under his influence that I made the decision to become vegetarian. Like Knox and Charlie before me, my normal teenage discontent had been channeled, upon the suggestion of a wacky poetry teacher, away from simple morosity and depression towards idealistic, moderately productive ends.

The reality, of course, is that 99% of teenage rebelliousness plays itself out along extremely well-worn channels—liking music that older people describe as "noise", getting stupid haircuts, and covertly smoking in bathrooms, among other things. There is significant irony in the fact that those kids whose identities are the most tied up in "non-conformism" are much more alike than the supposed "conformists" (yes, this means you, mopey, poetic soul who dresses all in black; crazy-dyed-Mohawk-and-piercings guy; and all of you "true originals" who are covered in tattoos... kind of like all of the other "true originals"[19]). And yet, forget what you may have heard about opposable thumbs, hunting in bands, or the development of language; it is the smug stupidity of teenagers who believe, against all evidence or reason, that their ideas are better than everybody else's that makes social evolution possible.

After fighting the current all the way back from the deep ocean to its breeding ground to spawn, a salmon can expect no greater reward than to die and be eaten by its indifferent offspring like so much bonito flakes[20]. Similarly ignominious are the events accompanying the final stage of many human lives as well: the nursing homes[21], the colostomy bags, the being weirdly patronized as if you've magically become five years old again...

While all of this probably pretty much sucks for the individual person (or fish) experiencing it, in Darwinian terms, it actually makes a lot of sense. Through the simple expedient of viewing their elders as completely boring, stupid, and more or less viscerally repulsive, members of the younger generation are free to look at the world with fresh eyes and to replace outdated ideologies with new ones.

---

19 in the interest of full disclosure, I should probably mention that in high school I was one of those kids who always wore an interesting hat

20 I realize that "bonito flakes" kind of sounds like a brand of Mexican breakfast cereal; it's actually a kind of fish food

21 aptly described by my sister, Zoe, as a lot like college: you have a roommate, you eat in a dining hall and, when you finally get out, they hold a ceremony that your whole family attends

The abolitionist movement, just as an example, was not founded by elderly slaveholders who spontaneously began to feel guilty about the way they made their living; it was started by starry-eyed young idealists who looked at the world around them, identified an injustice, and sought to remedy it.

Just a few minutes before sitting down to write this paragraph, I was flipping through one of those Village Voice-style tabloid newspapers that every city has[22] and happened to notice a listing for an upcoming "Concert Against Discrimination". There may be lingering racial issues yet to be resolved in this country, but let me ask you: when was the last time you saw a listing for a "Concert *For* Discrimination"? Things may still not be absolutely perfect just yet, but even the crankiest, most complainingest liberal out there has to admit that we've come a long way over the past few centuries.

Of course, not every so-called "youth movement" is so successful in becoming mainstream; on the contrary, the vast majority flame out within a single generation. Take, for example, the hippies—easily the grubbiest (both figuratively and literally) youth movement in recent history:

There's nothing at all wrong with some of their big ideals—ending wars, getting more in touch with oneself through transcendental meditation and hallucinogenic drugs, etc. The problem is that they muddled their message by packaging this

---

22 those weekly papers that are ostensibly dedicated to keeping you up to date on cultural events, but which are really just there to constantly remind you that, no matter what you do, you can never hope to be anywhere near as hip as its writers and editors

with some completely unrelated practices—never getting a haircut and smelling terrible, e.g.—as well. These extraneous characteristics are not at all appealing to regular people and only serve to cloud their perception of hippies and the anti-war movement. This is why, whereas the word "abolitionist" stirs up an essentially noble and romantic image, "hippie" has entered the lexicon as a more or less derogatory term.

People, in general, are vaguely in favor of morality and justice, *but they are not remotely interested in letting their freak flag fly.*

As things are currently situated, veganism appeals mainly to idealistic young people and those who, for one reason or another, have retained the mindset of this particular stage of life. By very definition, vegans are people who don't mind being seen as "freaky" or different; on the contrary, we more than likely derive a tremendous amount of pride and sense of self from such appellations.

As much of our personal identity is tied up in being a member of the "vegan community" we feel a conflicted interest to, on the one hand, win new converts while, on the other, to protect our elite status as Vegans™ from being watered down. To this end, we continually raise the standards and seek out new ways to "out-vegan" one another. Raw foodies, as an example, often pride themselves on having taken veganism "to the next level": a ridiculous affectation unless, unbeknownst to me, heating vegetables does, in fact, turn them into animals. When someone is set upon by the "vegan police" for some real or imagined infraction, we sit back quietly, basking in our own superiority for having avoided such transgressions—or perhaps afraid that if we speak up and attempt to restore sanity to the situation, we'll become the next victim ourselves.

If veganism is ever going to attain widespread acceptance, normal people need to look at our movement and not see a bunch of crazy freaks following a set of arbitrary rules in order to win a stupid, childish self-purity contest that no one with a job/family/life/normal set of values can ever be reasonably expected to having any interest in entering.

* * *

I was once out at a bar with some vegan friends when a couple of guys at a nearby table overheard our conversation—which was of course about veganism: the one and only topic that vegans ever discuss with each other[23]. I would have to conjecture that they were probably not in town for a Mensa meeting, and, on top of that, they'd been drinking. "You know what I could go for right now?" one of them asked the other, loudly, trotting out the old tried and true cliché. "A big juicy hamburger." And thus, emphatically, the moral position that meat is unethical due to its lack of juiciness was thoroughly refuted.

As a general rule, I don't see much point in engaging drunk people in a serious debate, not only because their temporary mental incapacity is likely to render such an endeavor pointless, but also because I am rarely around

---

23 have you noticed that too? Come on, people, what do you think God invented sports, politics and weather for?

drunk people except when I am drunk myself. What seems like a devastatingly waggish rejoinder on a Saturday night all too often turns out, in the cold light of Sunday morning, to have been something like "shut up, doo doo head" and then bursting into tears. Yet a particularly outspoken member of my party decided to seize upon this opportunity to attempt to disabuse these guys of their misconceived notion that vegans are wacky extremists at whose expense drunkards in bars may feel free to poke fun.

"I'm very psychic and intuitive," she explained, with an unbecoming hauteur. "And it is my belief that everything in the world has its own resonant energy. *Including this table.*" And thus began what was quite possibly the worst defense of veganism ever attempted. Building upon the premise that *table* abuse is wrong (and who could possibly disagree with that?) she logically reasoned that *animal* abuse—due to the self-evident fact that animals possess a higher "energy resonance" than do beer-soaked barroom tables—must therefore be even worse. Imagine, if you will, an anti-death penalty activist arguing from the position that if you would consider it immoral to administer a lethal injection to a *table* (and who wouldn't?) then you have even greater reason to refrain from doing so to a human being; or a gay rights activist who premised their argument on an assumed agreement that it would be unethical to deny *barroom tables* the right to marry. By the time her harangue was complete, these guys literally had tears in their eyes from laughing and even I had to admit that, by comparison, their argument "I could go for a juicy hamburger right now" was sounding downright perspicacious.

Now, I am a believer in a policy of tolerating differing opinions to the extent that I don't think that heretics ought to be burned at the stake. Freedom of religion is one of the fundamental rights upon which this country was founded and I support it implicitly, even to the point of taking the side of the crazy Christians when they argue that it is freedom of—as opposed to freedom from—religion that we are supposed to be guaranteed. So if someone wants to base their entire code of personal morality on the belief that tables have souls, I am certainly not going to call for their excommunication from the vegan movement. Yet at the same time, neither am I going to stand by and allow the impression to be made that ethical veganism is inherently based upon a patent absurdity if I can at all help it.

"Forget," I said to the two guys who could really go for juicy hamburgers, after waiting until my psychic, intuitive friend's attention was safely diverted, "everything she just said. That whole argument about the table? Quite possibly the single most ridiculous thing I have ever heard in my entire life." Very quickly, I outlined my own reasons for being vegan: a) animals are capable of feeling pain, b) we live in a world in which we have an abundance of food choices, and c) I feel better about myself choosing to eat things that don't inflict pain on other animals. There is nothing remotely profound about this explanation, and keep in mind that I delivered it in a drunken slur about two centimeters from their faces. Nonetheless, I think that I can most accurately characterize their reaction as one of astonishment. Whatever preconceived notions these guys might have had about vegans, they were apparently much less surprised to hear some nonsense about tables having souls than my hocus-pocus-free explanation about preferring not to hurt animals when given the choice.

I don't think it's highly likely that either of them rushed home that night and started researching tofu recipes on the Internet, but they shook my hand and seemed genuinely appreciative of the new perspective. Who knows what effect this may have somewhere down the line? Maybe someday one of these guys will have a teenage daughter who will announce at dinner one night her intention to become vegetarian. I think that we can agree that "oh, she's just trying to exercise her freedom to do a nice thing for animals," would be a much better perspective for her father to have in this circumstance than "oh, she must believe that tables have spirits inside of them".

Jesus

I have partaken of the rite of Holy Communion precisely one time in my life, though in an Episcopal—rather than in a Catholic—church. This might explain why the holy wafer tasted distinctly like a regular wafer and hardly at all like a tiny piece of a 2000-year-old corpse. Whereas other Christian groups have taken the eminently reasonable step of designating the wafers as merely symbolic of the body of Christ, if not dispensed with this ritual entirely, the Roman Catholic church alone still officially promotes the doctrine of transubstantiation, i.e., that upon coming into contact with human saliva, these crackers are literally transformed into a chunk of Jesus Christ's actual body. Think about this: there are around one billion Catholics in the world today, all of whom believe in a god that takes on four distinct forms— the father, the son, the holy ghost, and a special kind of snack food that's served in church on Sundays in order to tide you over until brunch.

I guess it really shouldn't be too surprising from the religion that also brought us the Crusades, but, in my opinion, the ritual of the Holy Sacrament is way more disturbing than the worst maggoty sheep testicle eating stunt that has ever appeared on Fear Factor. Not only does it constitute cannibalism, it is in point of fact the cannibalism of a guy who has been dead since the year 33—somewhere around 24,000 months longer than meat is normally expected to remain fresh, even under the most ideal of storage conditions. More troubling still, Catholics believe that in observing this ritual, they are carrying out the will of God: Jesus's own dad! Joe Rogan, host of Fear Factor, may sometimes tell contestants to eat, say, the moldy eyeballs of an alligator, but has he ever made anyone eat the body of his own long-dead son? No. Because Joe Rogan is not a raging psychopath.

If the doctrine of transubstantiation requires refutation, then I suggest that we need look no further than the fact that they make special wheat-free communion wafers for people with food allergies. I mean, was Jesus made out of wheat? If people with a wheat intolerance react to the Host in the exact same way that they do to, say, a toaster waffle (and not, for example, in the way that they would to a tiny piece of King Tut) then the obvious implications seem fairly difficult to avoid. If you were to add cinnamon and some confectioner's glaze to the basic holy wafer recipe, you might be able to come up with some kind of bun that you could eat with a cup of coffee, but to create a chunk of Jesus Christ's literal flesh by adding some mystical Latin incantations to same??

Magical crackers that turn into some guy's body when you eat them are something that J.K. Rowling wouldn't put in a novel due to plausibility issues.

Let's pretend for a moment that we live in a world in which transubstantiation is not a part of the doctrine of a major religion. I have just walked up to you on the street and offered you some food.

"What's in it?" you ask.

"Oh, flour, water, salt…" I answer vaguely. "But, oh yeah: when you put it in your mouth it turns into Jesus."

You'd think that I was a raving lunatic. And, even if you did somehow believe me, does this sound like something you'd really want to eat? On the contrary, I imagine a big slapstick spit take in which a big spray of cracker crumbs shoots out of your mouth when I tell you that you're eating human flesh. That's the other thing about the Eucharist that's kind of weird when you really think about it: why would anyone ever want to eat Jesus in the first place? I mean, Buddhists don't feel compelled to eat Buddha and, from the statues, he appears to have been downright succulent.

Catholics passively accept the idea that they are literally consuming little scraps of Jesus's body, washing it down with a sip of his blood from a communal chalice (eww!) because they are inured to the idea of it, and it just seems normal to them.

Likewise, people don't eat meat because they are evil or stupid or selfish or too ignorant to know that it's made from animals, but simply because to do so is a normal, accepted part of our culture.

They key to success for the vegan movement is to make veganism normal and accepted as well. This means: presenting ourselves as normal people who have made a reasonable choice for a sensible, logical reason—we must no longer sit back and let the overzealous, radical nutcases speak for the rest of us. This means: vegan shoe manufacturers making shoes that one might feel comfortable wearing to work, or to the gym, or for a night out on the town—not just to a be-in or hippie drum circle. This means: vegan cheese slices that actually taste like cheese—not like old, sweaty, discarded insoles. This means: when someone walks into a vegan restaurant and orders lasagna, they need to be served a plate with something remotely resembling lasagna on it—not some kind of new age raw "lasagna" made out of lentil sprouts and grated carrot.

In his book *Collapse*, evolutionary biologist Jared Diamond spoke of a very interesting experiment in which customers at a Home Depot were given a choice between buying plywood that was labeled as being environmentally friendly or plywood that was not (for control purposes—to prevent customers from making their decision based on quality—both the labeled and unlabeled wood were actually from the identical source). When the price was the same, the "environmentally friendly" wood outsold the other by about 2 to 1. And yet when the price of the "environmentally friendly" wood was increased by even 2%, this ratio was reversed. The obvious conclusion: most people vaguely prefer the psychological reward of doing the right thing, yet the majority is willing to give up essentially nothing in order to get it.

It is simply too much to ask that people pay more in order to be vegan, that they give up flavors they enjoy, or even that they sacrifice the sense of themselves as regular members of society. Veganism will become mainstream the day we figure out how to remove these obstacles and not a moment sooner.

* * *

A couple of thousand years ago there was a Jewish guy named Saul of Tarsus who liked to stone Christians to death. He just liked it; I don't know why. Then, through some set of circumstances, he had a change of heart and decided to become the founder of modern Christianity. The details here are unimportant. "Jesus is the messiah," Saul started telling his Jewish neighbors. "Ergo, it is consistent with the Jewish faith to believe in him. If we do, we'll go to Heaven."

"Or maybe," they answered him, "Jesus is just some crazy, bearded drifter with a messianic complex—kind of like Charles Manson or that guy who kidnapped Elizabeth Smart. And, either way, we're already going to Heaven anyway. 'Chosen people'? Ever heard of it? Ergo, believing in Jesus is pointless. And hey: aren't you that guy who used to like to stone Christians to death?"

"Jesus *is* the messiah," Saul would insist.

"I wish you could hear how stupid you sound right now, Saul," the Jews would respond.

Frustrated, Saul changed his name to Paul (which I suppose sounds less Jewish or something) and took his message to the pagans instead. Whereas Christianity had previously been considered a subset of Judaism (so that if any pagan wished to become Christian, he first had to become Jewish—which meant that he had to adopt strict Jewish dietary laws and undergo the single most horrifying operation of all time: adult circumcision), Paul's great innovation was to establish it as an independent religion in its own right. "Accept Jesus," Paul told the pagans, "and you can have eternal life. And you can keep on eating pork if you want to."

"And...?" said the pagans, slightly embarrassed. "What about... you know... down there?"

"Yes, yes. Fine," said Paul, setting down his *bris milah* blade with just a hint of disappointment. "You don't have to do that either."

The pagans had seen the world as an unpredictable and often cruel place and had constructed a cosmology that incorporated and attempted to make sense of this rogue element. Accordingly, they postulated the existence of a set of gods who were little more than emotionally ill alcoholics with anger control issues. Though this provided plenty of latitude to explain the ups and downs of daily existence, it also made their lives rather stressful. Imagine having Naomi Campbell as one of your deities, and having to juggle rituals designed to appease her with similar rituals for Russell Crowe, Sean Penn, and dozens of other crazy, pain-in-the-ass gods. You'd never be able to make them all happy at the same time and would constantly be dodging thunderbolts from someone or other. The appeal of swapping this kind of schizophrenic chaos for a kindly, paternalistic god and everlasting life is obvious. Of course, the Jews had *always* offered them a way to get into Heaven; Paul's marketing breakthrough was simply to lower the admission price—to remake the religion into something that better fits into the completely non-radical, humdrum existence of the common dung beetle.

What is Vegan?

German philosopher, and noted pompous ass, Georg Wilhelm Friedrich Hegel declared history to be at an end in 1806. Building upon the accumulated wisdom of the world's greatest thinkers from the time of the ancient Greeks on forward, Hegel—according to Hegel—had finally figured everything out. The progression of human consciousness was—according to Hegel—nothing more than the evolution of God towards full actualization. And the full actualization of God would be achieved at the point at which human consciousness recognized that God would become actualized when human consciousness recognized that that was how it would take place (I know it sounds circular, but it's really just pompous). All of recorded history—according to Hegel—was leading up to the one triumphant moment that he, Hegel, finally unraveled that mystery. As of 1806, God was fully actualized, and all of the questions of the universe had their answers. So what else was there? History was done.

Of course, Hegel's bones have been lying in the cold ground for the past couple of hundred years, and human thought has continued to evolve just that same as before. Possibly Hegel miscalculated slightly. Although most of us aren't likely to make this same mistake on such a grand scale, some modified version of this shortsightedness tends to be fairly chronic. We laugh at the mistakes of those who came before us with barely a thought of the fact that those who come after will be laughing at us in the same way. Throughout history, people continually misidentify themselves as the end result of a long evolutionary process instead of correctly seeing themselves as occupying a random point along a continuum. As a movement, we have made great strides over the years. But we make a big, fat, pompous, Hegelian mistake if we assume that we have reached the culmination of all that "vegan" can ever be.

* * *

"Are you familiar with Plato?" I once asked a girl, apropos of nothing.

"Of course!" she had answered, encouraging me with her responsiveness. Yet as I plowed forward with my semblance of a point ("Well, as he wrote in his *Meno* dialogue..."), I was met with an increasingly blank expression.

"Oh!" she finally interrupted, with unmasked scorn, "I thought you asked if I was familiar with *Play-Doh*."

Most of the early dialogues of Plato (the ancient Greek philosopher, not to be confused with the pleasantly-scented modeling clay) follow a very rigid format. Socrates, a scruffy old man with a Ted Kaczynski haircut (at least that's how I picture him) engages a very important and knowledgeable person in a conversation about their area of expertise. "What is justice?" he might, for example, ask of an ancient Hellenic version of Johnny Cochran.

The first answer he receives is generally rather succinct and intuitive, the kind of definition that we usually take as common sense, but Socrates is never satisfied with a simple explanation. In the guise of someone who is too stupid to understand what appears obvious to everyone else, he proceeds to interrogate the supposed expert, pointing out the inconsistencies and exceptions in whatever answers they give, forcing them to repeatedly amend and stretch their definition until they eventually contradict one of their initial premises and the whole theory collapses in a big confused heap.

Socrates' point all along was never to learn the definition at all, but to humble those who pretend to know more than they do. True wisdom, according to the Socratic tradition, lies not in the accumulation of facts, but in recognizing the limits of one's own knowledge.

In later dialogues, of course, Plato started to get all metaphysical and wrote a bunch of stuff about a bizarre, heavenly world inhabited by perfect, idealized horses living in perfect, idealized stables and eating perfect, idealized hay... but that stuff is downright Charlie Manson crazy. I'm not going to defend any of that. I am simply trying to point out that most of the definitions that most of us use to define veganism for ourselves most of the time would fall apart just as easily under this kind of scrutiny. We don't have as firm a grasp on it as we think we do.

Socrates: I am such a feeble-minded old man, and you are said to be so wise in matters such as this. I hear the word "vegan" used, but as much thought as I have given to it, I find myself thoroughly unable to grasp what is meant by it.

Us: It's simple. It means not eating anything that is derived from animals: meat, dairy, eggs, etc.

Socrates: This is what I've been told, but, once more, please forgive me, my poor old brain leaks like a sieve. I may be completely wrong about this, in fact I'm sure I am, but I seem to remember having heard it said that vegans also do not wear leather or fur. And just now you have told me that veganism has to do with what food one eats.

Us: Right. Well, it actually means living in such a way that we cause no harm to animals. So we don't eat any animal products, and we also don't wear them.

Socrates: I am sure that this answer would be perfectly satisfactory to one who is younger and more intelligent that I am, but with my advanced Alzheimer's, it's sometimes difficult for me to keep things straight. This may have been a dream or a hallucination, but I also having the nagging feeling that I may have been told by another vegan, but undoubtedly one not nearly so wise as you, that using products that are made by companies that test on animals is also anti-vegan.

Us: Yes. We don't do anything to harm animals in *any* way.

Socrates: A thousand times thank you for taking the time to explain this to me. As a baby, rocks were dropped on my head repeatedly, and I'm afraid to say that the experience may have had some negative consequences pertaining to my ability to reason clearly. Again, pardon me for taking up your time with what must undoubtedly seem like silly questions to one of your advanced knowledge and wisdom. But if you can find it in your heart to give just another moment of your precious time to a brain-damaged old moron, I am still not clear on your meaning. You have said that a vegan is one who does no harm to animals, yet just now I have seen you—whose reputation as the finest of vegans is widely known—drive up in a car.

Us: Uh-huh. So?

Socrates would go on to question us on how driving a car can be considered an acceptable part of the vegan lifestyle if the tires and pavement contain animal products, the roads usurp habitat space, and the mining and manufacturing processes as well as the car's exhaust system itself contribute to poisoning the natural environment (to make no mention of roadkill). If our goal is to reduce suffering, then why are we so strict about what we eat and a few other areas in which we impact animals (leather, fur, cosmetics, shampoo...), while ignoring or rationalizing other areas in which our impact is as great if not greater? Who gets to decide that eating minor animal byproducts like lactic acid, which does not drive an industry and contributes very insignificantly to the profitability of slaughtering animals, is inherently anti-vegan, but when it comes to something as destructive as driving a car, we have some leeway? Why do we reflexively boycott any company that tests on animals or sells fur, including those products that aren't tested or made of fur themselves, but consider it normal and acceptable (sometimes even preferable) to buy vegetarian meals at restaurants that also sell meat?

Many of us have dedicated our whole lives to veganism, yet under the microscope any pretense to fully comprehend it inevitably falls to pieces. Some, in an attempt to be as inclusive as possible, include *all* animals within their sphere of moral concern. Although this is certainly well-intentioned, what this actually amounts to is not objectivity, but the surrendering of a difficult and necessarily subjective ethical decision to Linnaeus ("the father of taxonomy"); less kindly, it could actually be *called kingdomist*, like racist or speciesist[24], except with a broader circle. As with any of the other "-isms", kingdomism is simply when we define a certain radius around ourselves—in this case, all animals and no non-animals—and assign moral agency based on inclusion or exclusion, rather than examining the personal merits of those individuals under consideration.

When we are thinking about a chimpanzee and a tree, the difference between animals and plants seems clear and obvious, but it would be much more difficult to explain just how and why the first proto-animal inherently valued its life more than the first proto-plant, or why a sea anemone has a built-in right to live while an anemone does not[25]. There

---

24 a term coined by Peter Singer to describe that bias which results in our performing medical experiments on apes yet not on Terri Schiavo
25 a sea anemone is a brainless animal that resembles a mushroom; an anemone is a

is nothing about the specific historical moment at which the plant and animal lineages diverged that makes it inherently any more important than any other minor mutation. It is simply the spot where human scientists found it expedient to draw the line. Can we really trust our taxonomists to have also, by sheer coincidence, chosen the exact right point at which moral agency begins and leaves off as well? Is ethical standing really best determined by whether our cells have a cellulose wall around the membrane?

Anti-scientific creationists love to use the example of the eye to try to discount evolution: "If evolution proceeds by slow degrees based on the usefulness of the intermediate forms, how could something as complex as the eye have evolved? What's the use of 5% of an eye?" The answer, of course, is that being able to detect light in some rudimentary form is better than not being able to detect it at all; being able to focus an image slightly is better than not having any capability. Recently there were stories circulating that Stevie Wonder was considering undergoing experimental surgery that could give him the ability to detect light and shadow, but not to see images. Maybe we should ask him what good 5% of an eye is. Rather than be troubled over how something as "perfect" as the eye could have been developed through a process as messy as evolution, eminent evolutionary biologist Ernst Mayr actually speculated that eyes may have evolved as many as 40 independent times in separate species. Cephalopods like octopi and squid, for example, have eyes remarkably similar to our own, yet other

flower

members of their phylum (e.g, oysters and mussels) and our most recent common ancestors have no eyes at all. It seems that our eyes and the eyes of a cuttlefish are similar not because of common origin, but because of *convergent evolution*. Should this surprise us? Evolution approaches every problem the same way; it throws everything in its entire bag of tricks at it until finds something that works. In the presence of similar pressures working with similar raw materials, why shouldn't similar adaptive structures or capabilities evolve?

I am sure we have all been confronted by meat-eaters who claim to believe that plants feel pain and have consciousness, and who attempt to justify their meat-eating by saying that causing suffering to living creatures is unavoidable no matter what you eat. This is an absurd, desperate argument because plants, in general, have little adaptive advantage in being able to feel pain, and there is a complete lack of scientific evidence to suggest that they do. Yet, for argument's sake, we must at least admit the *possibility* of sentience evolving in a kingdom other than our own. Evolution created consciousness (at least) once; it could certainly do it again. The fatal flaw of the kingdomist viewpoint is that it would exclude even a walking, talking Mr. Potato Head from moral consideration based solely upon its relatedness to us. Of course, this is taking the argument ad absurdum, and I'm sure most vegans who purport to respect the rights of all animals would protest "that's not what I meant when I drew the line there!" Of course not. What you meant was that it is the characteristics normally present in animals and absent in plants that are morally relevant. If a plant could be proven to have sentience, *of course* you would respect its right to life. The kingdom assigned to an organism by our taxonomists is a foolish ethical criterion.

Recognizing this fact, many vegans follow Peter Singer in attempting to draw the moral divide between those organisms capable of having personal "interests" (i.e., those with the ability to feel pain and care about themselves) and those that do not. This system would include sentient plants (if any existed), and exclude insentient animals (because it is logically impossible to inflict suffering on an organism that is incapable of suffering, whatever kingdom it is in), basing morality upon objective criteria instead of leaving it up to taxonomists to determine. While this is a much more logical and thoughtful approach, the difficulty lies in the impossibility of determining exactly which creatures have "interests" and which don't.

Vegans who eat honey do not do so because they hate bees and want them to suffer as much as possible; it is simply their belief that bees do not have the capability of suffering. And who's to say that they're wrong? When we are talking about relatively close relatives like mammals, or even vertebrates in general, it is easy to make the argument that if an animal has a physiologically similar nervous system to our own, and reacts to a painful stimulus in the same way that we would, they are most likely experiencing the same pain that we would in the same situation. But this does not hold true with insects. They can lose a leg and not even flinch; they can be cut in half and each half will still go about its business more or less as usual. Their nervous systems are so different from ours that if they have a pain mechanism at all, it is unrecognizable to us. Many would argue that it is safer to err on the side of caution and act as though we believe that they do feel pain. Others feel that the bulk of evidence makes it safe enough to assume that they don't. After all, we can't really prove *anything*. We can't prove that doorknobs don't feel pain when we turn them. We are just operating on what common sense and the extent of knowledge that we do have tells us. Both of these arguments have a certain merit.

Even if there were a perfect method of determining which species are deserving of our concern and which aren't, attempting to define exactly what constitutes mistreatment or exploitation opens up another can of worms (no offense) altogether. Even when we are talking about the one species whose right to life is almost universally accepted—our own—there are fundamental issues, such as abortion rights, that are far from settled. Although we may disparagingly refer to one another as "pro-death" or "anti-choice", neither group thinks of themselves that way. No one hates unborn babies and wants them to be murdered; they simply don't believe that in the early stages of pregnancy a fetus has personal "interests" yet. Conversely, no one wants to strip women of their rights on principle alone; it is simply their belief that every human blastocyst has a right to continue developing that is even more unalienable.

I have met several people whose bond with horses was their pathway to becoming vegan and, while they see no conflict in continuing to ride, other vegans are uncomfort-able with the idea. There are vegans who think that letting cats go outside is cruel (it exposes them to dangers with which they are not adequately equipped to deal, and they wreak havoc on wildlife) and others who think that the exact opposite is the case—that restricting their freedom by *not* letting them go outside is cruel. Some vegans object to the idea of keeping "pets" at all, while many of us see it as our moral responsibility to provide shelter for as many homeless animals as we possibly can. Maybe the problem is that we are trying to identify a single point at which morality can be cleanly separated from immorality, a point at which we are completely faultless in every way, when reality is far too messy and paradoxical to allow such a point to exist.

When we look at it closely, it is clear that living in such a way as to cause absolutely no harm to animals is impossible. If it's not driving a car, it's using energy, or living in a house where there was once animal habitat, or eating wild berries and thereby depleting the food supply of cedar waxwings. The fact is, you can't even shoot yourself in the middle of the forest without giving lead poisoning to the pack of coyotes who eat you and probably crushing a bug when you fall. This is not to say that all of our choices are morally *equal* (just because the concept of pure justice is impossible to com-pletely capture in real life, it doesn't make it any less obvious that the OJ verdict was a joke), but we should realize that when we define vegan as "causing no harm", we are talking about a purely theoretical, unattainable ideal. By this defini-tion, John freaking Robbins isn't vegan either.

I have also seen vegan defined as "a striving" to avoid suffering, or as avoiding contributing to suffering "as much as possible". While these amendments acknowledge and attempt to address the impossibility of living (or dying) without affecting animals negatively in some ways, they are ultimately meaningless. Who's to say how much striving is enough, or how much is really possible? Consider a ridiculous hypothetical: what if a person genuinely cares about animals and does everything in their power to minimize their contribution to suffering, yet has a bizarre psychological addiction to hamburgers that they are simply unable to overcome despite all of their striving? According to this open-ended definition, this person would have to be considered to be vegan—they do as much as is personally possible to help animals, yet I don't think many of us would be comfortable calling them that.

Ultimately, no definition of veganism is ever going to be perfect. The best we can do is to remember that, whichever version we settle upon for ourselves, it wasn't handed down to some guy named Moses on a mountaintop. The way I look at it, any definition of veganism is as good as any other provided it places the emphasis where it belongs: on the effect something has on animals, rather than on one's own personal purity.

* * *

Many years ago, I went to visit my friend, Gus, who was working as caretaker of a ranch way out somewhere in the

Grand Teton mountains of Wyoming. It was an idyllic place that perhaps even Laura Ingalls might have described as quaint and old-fashioned. There was no electricity—everything was cooked on a wood-burning stove, beer was chilled by tying a rope to it and throwing it in the stream, and crapping was done in a two-seater outhouse. The few farm animals in residence had been left behind by the previous owner and were all retired.

The cows, Gus told me, were free to come and go as they pleased. In wintertime, they mostly stuck close to the ranch, taking advantage of the warm barn and all-you-can-eat hay, while in the summer they would often be gone for weeks at a time; occasionally, he would catch a glimpse of them running through the forest. The half-dozen or so chickens, as well, enjoyed about as ideal a situation as you could ever hope for them: plenty of food, unrestricted access to the outdoors, and a nice, safe, coyote-free place to sleep. Gus's plan was to keep feeding them until they had died of old age.

One morning, while I was still sleeping, Gus got up and fixed some sourdough pancakes, using a couple of chicken eggs. Schmuckily enough, I became self-righteously indignant and refused to eat them—not because I thought eating eggs was disgusting (although I do), but because I was clinging to a religious view of veganism that ultimately makes no sense. Although I agreed with his reasoning that the chickens—who, being chickens, lay unfertilized eggs as a matter of course—would not be damaged in any way if I ate the pancakes, I nonetheless insisted that it wouldn't be "vegan" of me to do so. Thus, I neatly reduced "veganism" to an absurdity, made myself look like a confused fool who doesn't even understand his own deeply held convictions, and was a rude and ungrateful houseguest all at the same time.

Beware of definitions of veganism that prohibit behaviors that don't actually have a negative impact on animals... and those, as well, that permit behaviors that do...

"Gwagwagwe"

I have a good friend named Jay. Let me start that again: I used to have a good friend who used to be named Jay. At some point, he changed his name to "Gwagwagwe" (the significance of which eludes me), and sort of dropped out of society. I haven't heard from him in a number of years.

It is disappointing, if not surprising, to learn that many of the people entrusted to make decisions concerning wild animal populations are the very same people who shoot them as a form of recreation. Jay, the only other vegan in the wildlife science program with me when I was in college, never missed an opportunity to point out the hypocrisy. He had a particular radar for the trade euphemisms that are commonly employed to mask bloody realities (like "harvest" when what you really mean is "murder in cold blood"), and had no reservations about sharing his opinions with anyone (e.g., our professors) at any time (e.g., while guaranteeing himself a D- on a final exam essay).

Most people adopt a personal philosophy that amounts to little more than a rationalization of all the things they want to be doing anyway. Jay almost had the opposite fault: he was constantly reevaluating his position in the world and radically changing his viewpoint from one moment to the next. He had been a communist warrior before I met him and was arrested for the ultimate in symbolic crimes: assaulting a police officer with an American flag. While we were in school together, he was a hardcore animal rights activist with the same vague intentions that I had: to infiltrate the system and change it from within. Then he became "Gwagwagwe" and his perspective was that going along with the conventional rules of society to any extent at all was to perpetuate an unfair system. "Gwagwagwe" didn't feel so good about paying taxes or rent or... anything else. "Gwagwagwe" was all about roaming the country, ceremonially burning sagebrush and things. Most notably, while Jay had always followed a strict vegan diet, "Gwagwagwe" was a meat-eater.

I remember when I was a little kid and those signs outside of the McDonald's restaurants used to be periodically updated. They were actually keeping track of how many billions had been served. When 4 billion was no longer accurate, they changed it to 4.5, as if that additional 500,000,000 would be enough to persuade skeptical passersby who were unimpressed by a measly 4,000,000,000. Now, depressingly enough, they've maxed out the old signs at "over 99 billion", and the newer ones avoid the issue altogether by simply saying billions and billions served. I've never really been entirely clear on whether that represents the number of customers they've served, or the number of hamburgers they've served to customers, but either way the point is the same: they're counting the number *served*. It's not how many people have eaten there, or how many burgers have actually been ingested.

Although McDonald's is ostensibly in the restaurant business, whether or not their hamburgers actually end up in someone's digestive tract is a matter of complete indifference to them. If eating meat suddenly went out of style, while disposable cow flesh hockey pucks simultaneously came into vogue, how much would McDonald's really care? Their mission is not to alleviate hunger (or, for that matter, to kill as many animals and cause as much destruction as possible); they are in the business of making money, and it just so happens that marketing little patties of dead cow as food is an extremely efficient way of accomplishing that goal.

Of course, most of the time we buy what we eat and we eat what we buy, so not buying meat and not eating meat are usually one and the same. This is certainly how it was with Jay. But "Gwagwagwe" followed a slightly different path. Jay was the type to walk into a restaurant, place an order, eat the food that was set down before him, and not leave until he had paid. "Gwagwagwe" instead searched through dumpsters behind restaurants and ate whatever appeared to be edible, meat or otherwise, without paying a dime.

"Gwagwagwe"'s cholesterol was probably a little bit higher, and his risk of contracting the plague was increased significantly, but from a moral standpoint, he hadn't really changed. Although he was now eating animals, he still wasn't paying for them to be killed. Jay was a vegan; "Gwagwagwe" was freegan.

I avoid meat for ethical reasons. Same with dairy. And I also refuse to eat yams. This last one gets an asterisk, though, because it is only because I perceive yams to be horrible-tasting squishy orange crap. But as disgusting as I perceive them to be, I have no grounds to moralize about them. If you like to eat yams, then more power to you. Enjoy! Just don't expect me to kiss you afterwards.

And the same goes for old hamburgers found in the dumpster behind the McDonald's.

By the time a beef patty finds its way into the trash, every drop of potential profit has already been squeezed out of it. It might have been partially eaten and discarded by a customer. Or it might have been dropped on the floor by an employee and thrown out without having been sold (but only if a manager were watching when it happened; otherwise, it would have been brushed off, possibly spit upon, and then served anyway). Whatever a particular chunk of dead cow's story is, by the time it is out in the trash, it is no longer of any value to the restaurant. If "Gwagwagwe"'s digestive tract happens to intercept it on the way to the dump, they don't change the marquee from *infinity served* to *infinity plus one served*. They either sold it or didn't sell it, took their profit or wrote off their loss, prior to it getting thrown in there, a rat nibbling on it—also probably pooping on it a little bit—and "Gwagwagwe" coming along and eating whatever remains. The restaurant has already collected its money, and so have the meat distributor, slaughterhouse, rancher, livestock auction and everyone else involved in any step of the process. These people definitely care if a hamburger is *purchased*; it keeps the money flowing down the same path, giving them all a financial incentive to subject other cows to the same type of treatment. But none of them gives a damn if "Gwagwagwe" wants to eat a rat-poopy old hamburger out of a dumpster. And so the cows don't care. And so we shouldn't care.

So many times I have heard people shrug off responsibility for what their dogs and cats eat by referring to the cats and dogs' inherent lack of moral understanding. Cats and dogs, they argue, don't understand what they're eating is in actuality the dead bodies of other animals and, even if they did, they would probably be incapable of grasping the moral implications and empathizing with their suffering. By eating meat, therefore, the cats and dogs are not doing something immoral any more than a lion or a wolf acts immorally by eating meat.

I agree.

But we are.

There is a huge difference between a lion or a wolf killing and eating another animal, following an instinct and as a necessary means to survival, and a domestic cat or dog eating the bodies of animals that have been bred, raised, tortured, slaughtered, rendered, extruded, packaged, purchased and served by humans. Although we may feel sorry for the individual involved, it is difficult to say that anything immoral has happened when a weak gazelle is separated from the herd and taken down by a lion. This is simply a part of the natural predator/prey relationship between species that have been locked into a symbiotic relationship together over evolutionary time. Predation by lions helps prevent the gazelle population from outgrowing its food supply, and selective removal of weaker individuals maintains its genetic excellence. Ultimately, the gazelles are as dependent on the lions as the lions are on the gazelles.

The same relationship cannot be said to exist between the cats and dogs that live in our homes and the barely recognizable animals that have been turned into pellets or packed in cans that magically appear in their bowls twice a day. There is no dynamic, natural interaction that ultimately benefits both species. The animals we feed to our cats and dogs have been genetically manipulated, pumped full of hormones, confined, beaten, and murdered without ever having had a chance at a normal life. When they eat meat, it is not because they are following some immutable instinct that has developed over millions of years; it is simply because we have chosen to put some in their dish and they have learned to recognize it as food.

Dogs are natural scavengers; by design, they can easily adapt to eating almost anything. And cats, it should be noted, have a strong *hunting* instinct, but not an instinct to *eat meat*. All cats will chase and bat around small objects, twist-ties, mice, those little plastic rings from water jugs, etc., but it is only those who have been trained by their mothers during kittenhood to recognize some of these things as food who will actually eat what they have killed. The way to satisfy their natural hunting instinct, then, is not to feed them dead animal parts but to give them toys and play with them.

When our cats and dogs eat the meat-based foods that we have given them, a factory-farmed animal has had to suffer and die. A chicken has spent a short, tortured life in a crowded cage; a cow has been hung upside down on a conveyor belt and had her throat slit. Just because our cats and dogs don't understand this and can't be held morally responsible for it doesn't mean that no injustice has been committed!

Let's say I walk into a McDonald's, buy a hamburger, and then throw it into the trash without having taken a bite. If "Gwagwagwe" happens to come along later and eat it out of the dumpster, he has done nothing immoral. But does his lack of moral responsibility excuse my actions? Does it somehow not matter that a cow had to suffer and die in a slaughterhouse to produce a hamburger as long as the person whose intestinal tract it ultimately ends up in can't be held morally responsible? It makes no sense to think this way. If "Gwagwagwe" isn't ethically responsible for the suffering inherent in the meat he eats, that doesn't mean that it didn't happen, or that it doesn't matter. It simply means that we must look elsewhere to place the blame. In this case, it is obvious where it belongs: on the person who created consumer demand for the product of animal torture and mandated the continuation of the practices that produced it through their purchase. In other words, *me* (in my hypothetical example): the person who bought it. And so it is with the meat we give to our cats and dogs as well.

There is a loophole in our most common working definitions of veganism that allows us to be directly responsible for animals dying provided that we meet the arbitrary requirement of not actually putting them into our own mouths. But this is simply an imperfection in our definition; it is not a morally relevant distinction. *Why do we put the focus on ourselves (what we personally ingest, or wear on our own bodies), rather than where it belongs: on the animals (how they are affected by our actions), when to do so clearly misses the essential point of being vegan in the first place?*

Animal suffering is perpetuated just as surely whether we pay to eat animals, pay to wear them, pay and then inexplicably throw them in the dumpster, pay and then play a macabre game of hockey with them, or pay to feed them to our cats and dogs. So how can we possibly morally differentiate between these things? The slaughter industry doesn't decide to kill more animals at such point that meat enters our bodies, or when we slip into a pair of leather shoes: they kill animals when we *give them the financial incentive to do so.*

It doesn't matter one bit if you can make a lawyer's argument to excuse yourself from personal culpability when your cats and dogs eat meat; veganism isn't about you and your status within the community. The point of veganism is to reduce the amount of animal suffering in the world, not to reduce the amount for which you, personally, can be held accountable.

* * *

German philosopher, and noted pompous ass (aren't they all?), Immanuel Kant proposed a system of ethics based upon a precept called the Categorical Imperative:

> "Act only according to that maxim whereby you can at the same time will that it should become a universal law."

Have you ever noticed that pompous Germans always add about twelve unnecessary words to every sentence just to remove any risk that you might actually understand what they mean? Essentially, what Kant is saying is this: *consider what the result would be if everyone in the world acted exactly like you.*

It's a prototypically German philosophy as it idealizes homogeny in thought and action; nonetheless, I think it might be quite useful for vegans to consider a modified version of it.

Shoplifting, according to this rule, is unethical because if *everyone* did it, our economy would collapse and chaos would ensue[26].

Similarly, buying hamburgers ought to be considered to be unethical because, if everyone did it, cows would continue to be killed in order to fill the demand. On the other hand, eating a hamburger out of the dumpster is perfectly fine. If no one ate meat except that which they had found in the trash, the slaughter industry would quickly go bankrupt.

---

26 and, yes, this would be a bad thing. Think New Orleans immediately after Hurricane Katrina. Radical anarchism is a fun philosophy, but if you still believe in it after your 30th birthday, write to me and I'll send you a free t-shirt

Buying leather *new* is not acceptable. If everyone did that, the consequent demand would be enough to mandate continued exploitation of animals. Yet leather purchased at a secondhand store or left over from before one became vegan is no big deal. No animals would be harmed if everyone in the world restricted themselves exclusively to leather that was previously in circulation.

To buy cheese is contrary to a vegan ethic because universal support for the dairy industry would perpetuate great suffering. On the other hand, there is no mono and diglycerides industry. If everyone eschewed meat, dairy and eggs but didn't concern themselves with minor byproducts such as these, the animal slaughter industry would come crashing down just as surely as if we had. Hence—and I'm sure it freaks some people out to hear me say this—whether we worry about such things or not is a matter of complete indifference.

I oppose the practice of feeding meat to our cats and dogs for essentially this reason: if everyone stopped eating meat but continued to demand that meat be made available for their pets, the animal slaughter industry would continue to be profitable and animals would continue to suffer needlessly.

I do understand, however, that for most people this issue is not nearly so simple as this…

"Cats, Dogs..."

Yes! (It's Synthetic)

"No, I don't eat meat. Yes, I get enough protein. No, my shoes aren't leather. Yes, I have a life."

Sometimes you just know what questions are coming before they've even been asked. At a fur demo or similar pro-animal event, for example, a sign or t-shirt with the preceding preemptive response is almost certain to come in handy.

Throughout the duration of this book, I will be discussing the issue of vegetarianism in cats and dogs from a number of angles—examining several ethical arguments and looking into the possible health risks/benefits of both a vegan as well as a traditional meat-based diet. I believe that all of these topics have merit, as each attempts to address a misconception or area of concern that is common to many people.

Yet the reality is that just three words are probably more important than all that will follow put together: *Yes! (It's synthetic.)*

Did I answer your question?

I know, I know. Not everyone gets that. Some of you are sitting there right now, scratching your heads: "did you answer my what now?" But for a lot of you, I am Carnac the Magnificent. I am *Jeopardy* host Alex Trebek. I am Radar O'Reilly from *M*A*S*H*. I am TV psychic John Edward. *I am someone who you have heard of who knows the answers to things before they have even been asked.* But there's really no trick to it. In the years I sold vegan cat and dog food for a living, I answered the same question about the amino acid *taurine* hundreds—if not thousands—of times. At festivals and other public events, I often had the same conversation dozens of times in a single day. After a while, it becomes pretty easy to predict:

Does the vegan cat food contain taurine? *Yes! (It's synthetic.)*

Socrates is a man; all men are mortal; therefore, Socrates is mortal. If you ever took a logic course in school, you probably remember this example from the first five minutes of the first day of class. And if not, then welcome to Logic 101. There is nothing here to suggest that mortality was the only characteristic of Socrates (by all accounts, he was also smart, ugly, Greek and gay), or that other groups besides just men (e.g., chickens, dogs, women) might not be mortal as well. Yet once we've established the mortality of all men, it's clear that we can't very well turn around and claim that one of them will live forever. Socrates, logical man that he was, drank hemlock and promptly dropped dead.

Many people (including, unfortunately, some vegans, vegetarians and veterinarians) mistakenly believe that they are following a similar inescapable logic when they reach the conclusion that cats need to be given meat in order to fulfill their taurine requirement. A deficiency of taurine—or, as I so often hear it called, "that one thing that cats are supposed to need... you know what I mean..."—causes blindness and an ultimately fatal enlargement of the heart. While most humans, dogs, and other mammals can synthesize adequate amounts from methionine (which naturally occurs in beans, seeds and other plants) and cysteine (obtained from oats and broccoli, among other non-meat sources), cats are lacking in this ability and so require a preformed dietary source. Found in abundance in such appetizing places as organ meats, brains and eyeballs, taurine is not known to occur in any plant. *Cats need taurine*, the reasoning goes, *and taurine can be found in meat but not in plants. Therefore, cats need to eat meat.* (Actually, what people often say is "therefore, cats are *obligate carnivores*," as if this pseudo-authoritative phrasing automatically trumps "cats can be vegan" by virtue, I am guessing, of its Scrabble value alone.) Socrates' morality was a rock solid guarantee because the premises given essentially defined a world in which only three sets of characteristics were possible: "mortal men", "mortal non-men", and "non-mortal non-men", and had completely eliminated the possibility of "non-mortal men". The conclusion that cats need to eat meat in order to obtain dietary taurine, on the other hand, is based on no such logical necessity. While we are given enough information to narrow down our options somewhat (we know that taurine can't be found in the produce section), we are never told that meat is the only place it *can* be found. In other words, "non-meat, *plant*, containing taurine" has been eliminated as a possibility, but "non-meat, *non-plant*, containing taurine" has not.

The mistake is in not recognizing that the world is made up of more than just animals and plants.

Cows have—I can't remember the exact number, so let's just say, oh, I don't know—seven hundred cotillion stomachs (yes, I realize that a "cotillion" is a formal ball in which young ladies are presented to society, but it sounds like a really big number, doesn't it?), and somewhere in there, towards the mouth end, is a resident population of naturally-occurring gut bacteria that is able to produce all of the vitamin B12 that a cow could ever need. Other strictly herbivorous animals (e.g., rabbits) may keep their B12-producing microbes in their *lower* intestinal tract instead, and so utilize the always pleasant strategy of coprophagy (phagy=the eating of, copro=shit) to get their RDA of this vitamin.

We, however, have just the one stomach and consume human excrement only when it is covertly slipped to us by disgruntled fast food restaurant employees. So where is our B12 coming from then? Many vegans believe that as long as we intentionally do a bad job washing our vegetables, we'll somehow magically obtain enough from the bacteria in the remaining dirt to avoid the devastating mental deterioration that accompanies a deficiency. Unfortunately, this has never been shown to work out in real life (and, more to the point, *have you ever considered that the guy who works in the produce* section might pick his nose?). The fact of the matter is that we need a dietary source of B12 to be healthy, and that B12 is found in meat and other animal products but not reliably in plants—not even really dirty ones. In other words, B12 is to us as taurine is to cats. So why aren't we resigned to our own status as *obligate carnivores* (or at least *obligate omnivores*) as well?

When it comes to B12, more of us are probably actually guilty of underestimating the difficulty of getting enough in our diets. Crazier still than the dirt-eaters are the cheek-chewers—those who somehow believe that all the B12 we need is stuck to the insides of our own mouths already and that we just need to gnaw some off every once in a while. Even those who are a little bit more cautious find it easy enough to point to such things as fortified soy milks, cereals and nutritional yeasts as easy alternative sources from which this nutrient can be obtained; some may even resort to such extreme measures as taking a daily vitamin pill just to be safe. Whatever each of us does or does not do in order to ensure that we get enough B12, we all tend to at least have one thing in common: we generally don't worry about it too much. I'll bet that the first time you heard that B12 wasn't found in plants, you thought one of two things: "So I guess I'll live without B12 then" (which is actually not too smart, although I'll confess it's what I first thought), or "Then I'd better make sure I'm getting some of the synthetic version" (which is the more intelligent, reasonable thing to think). Either way, I'll bet you didn't think "Sounds like my hands are tied and I have to continue eating meat forever."

The fact that B12 can't be derived from plants doesn't lead any of us to the conclusion that veganism in humans is impossible.

Compared to some of the other everyday synthetics that we completely take for granted (e.g., hormone and brain chemical analogs like Prozac, Viagra, and birth control pills), creating something as mundane as a simple vitamin from inorganic sources almost sounds like a rainy afternoon project for an eight-year-old with a chemistry set. It would never even occur to us that it might be beyond our technological grasp. So why would we ever think that synthetically producing a simple amino acid like taurine would be any more difficult?

If Theodore Roosevelt had told you that taurine could only be derived from meat, he'd have been right. But that's only because he died in 1919. As long ago as the 1920's, the old method of isolating taurine from ox bile or abalone was already outdated, having been replaced by the more efficient process of creating it synthetically. Those with more intelligence and/or chemistry background than I have may find it instructive to hear this process described as the result of synthesis by sodium sulfite sulfonation of ethylene chloride followed by ammonolysis with anhydrous NH3 (ammonia without water) or with aqueous NH3 (ammonia with water) and ammonium carbonate.

Blah, blah, blah. I suspect that most people will agree with me in preferring the following dumbed down version instead: *stuff goes in; chemical changes occur as if by magic; taurine comes out.*

Today, taurine is a popular ingredient in energy drinks and bodybuilding supplements, and despite the nasty rumor that "Red Bull" got its name because its taurine is derived from bull testicles, it should be unsurprising that most companies use the cheaper and more readily available synthetic form. (Actually, the word "taurine" means "of or like a bull", just as "bovine" means "of or like a cow", so the brand name makes a lot of sense even without resorting to the bizarre testicle theory). Of course, taurine is a nonessential amino acid for humans and there are varying opinions on what it actually does for us (ranging from "miraculously curing all cardiovascular problems, alcoholism, and diabetes" to "possible mild placebo effect among certain highly suggestible individuals"). I'm not an expert, but the only noticeable effect on humans I've ever observed is its remarkable ability to make them spend way too much money on teeny tiny cans of crappy-tasting soda. Nonetheless, I hope the availability of synthetic taurine since the Woodrow Wilson administration, coupled with the ubiquity of products containing it on store shelves all around us today, is sufficient to erase an lingering "taurine can only be found in meat" nonsense. But I have to concede that none of this is a guarantee that the synthetic form will be metabolized by cats as efficiently as that which naturally occurs.

Many vets—those that are even aware that synthetic taurine exists at all, that is (and many do not, which is a scary thing)—will raise this as an objection. To be able to say with confidence that synthetic taurine is adequate, we'd want to be able to look at a large number of cats that have been fed synthetic taurine over a lifetime. Which is an easier sample to come by than they might imagine...

The greatest irony in this whole foolish taurine issue is the simple fact that most cats living today have been relying on synthetic taurine all of their lives anyway!

In the late 1980's, tens of thousands of regular old meat-eating cats were dying mysteriously each year from dilated cardiomyopathy (enlargement of the heart). Although these cats were far from vegan—they were being given a variety of popular brands of meat-based cat food, including many whose commercials you have seen and probably know by (enlarged?) heart—it was ultimately traced to a deficiency of taurine. At first glance, this seems counterintuitive: taurine, after all, is supposed to be found in meat. In fact, isn't that the whole reason why cats aren't supposed to be vegan in the first place?

The problem is that while historically, in nature, cats had no trouble deriving plenty of taurine from meat, historically, in nature, the "meat" they were eating was the whole bodies of raw, freshly-killed rodents, birds and insects with bellies full of enzymes. Whereas now "meat" refers to the byproducts of the animal slaughter industry, along with other assorted odds and ends, which have been mixed together and rendered at an extremely high temperature. Just as how soaking your laundry in hot water instead of cold causes blood stains to set, the high temperature of the rendering process was causing whatever was present at the outset to denature.

These days, most manufacturers of meat brands are aware of this potential deficiency, and compensate by adding taurine supplements after rendering is complete. These are the same companies that save money by supplementing their products with old, moldy grains and spoiled supermarket meats. Would it be reasonable to suppose that they've revived the more expensive, less efficient old ox bile/abalone method of taurine extraction for this purpose? Just as you'd expect, they make use of the cheapest and most readily available form (the synthetic one), which is exactly the same taurine that the vegan cat food manufacturers use.

The Aching-Ass Equation

There is currently a movement afoot to replace the words "pet" and "owner" in the legal language of laws and statutes, as well as in the common vernacular of everyday speech, with "companion animal" and "guardian". The idea is that improved treatment of animals will logically follow if we retrain our minds to think of them as individuals with inherent worth instead of as our property.

I'm not so sure I have a big problem with "pet". A "pet project" is a good thing, and "pet" is kind of an olde time term of endearment, along the lines of "dear" or "honey" (or is "honey" supposed to be offensive to vegans too?). I really don't see much of a negative connotation there; I just think it gets a bad rap because of its false pairing with "owner" (while the true, highly offensive, partner of "owner" is "possession", not "pet"). Also, I'm not convinced that "companion animal" is a great choice for a replacement. If we call them "companion" animals, doesn't that sort of define them solely as they relate to us, as if serving as companions to humans is their whole purpose for existing? This has a certain Rainbow Bridgeishness[27] to it with which I am not entirely comfortable.

Insofar as this movement seeks to strike down the word "owner", however, I support it 1,000,000% and in my opinion it would be difficult to find a more thoroughly appropriate substitute than "guardian". Right alongside "guardian angel", my immediate association with this word is from when I was an elementary school student. Maybe this is familiar to other people as well: at the bottom of every form we had to bring home to get signed—permission slips, report cards, etc.—there was a signature line, labeled not simply "Parent", but always "Parent/Guardian".

"Parent/Guardians" were the adults you lived with, who packed your lunch, paid for your clothes, yelled at you when you got bad grades, took you to the doctor when you were sick, loved you, guilt-tripped you, picked you up at the mall, embarrassed you in front of your friends. "Parents", of course, referred to the people whose sweaty lovemaking had directly brought you into existence. Most of us had at

---

27 there is a very famous poem called "Rainbow Bridge" that many people look to for comfort when a companion has died: "There are meadows and hills for all of our special friends so that they can run and play together. There is plenty of food, water and sunshine, and our friends are warm and comfortable. All the animals who had been ill and old are restored to health and vigor; those who were hurt or maimed are made whole and strong again, just as we remember them in our dreams of days and times gone by..." Doggie Heaven sounds really nice until you start looking at the strict and, I would say, arbitrary, entrance requirements: "When an animal dies *that has been especially close to someone here*, that pet goes to Rainbow Bridge" (italics mine). How unbelievably arrogant! Where are the ones who weren't lucky enough to have been close to someone here? Burning for all eternity in Doggie Hell (along with, according to Homer Simpson, Hitler's dog, Nixon's dog, and the mean Lassie that mauled Timmy)?

least one of those at home. But "Guardians" were the adults who took care of you if you didn't happen to have "Parents". The only difference was that they had come to be in charge of you by some other route.

Assuming sweaty lovemaking had little to do with bringing most of our cats and dogs into our lives (if your own story is an exception, I'd love to hear it), calling ourselves their "parents" is not strictly accurate; by using "guardian" though, we are able to capture the parental relationship without defying biological laws and coming off sounding silly.

To adopt a parental attitude towards our cats and dogs would be to recognize that we have the same set of commitments and responsibilities towards them as we do to our human children. A parent can't, for example, tie up a dependent child in the backyard and leave them there, or get rid of one who has become troublesome and replace them later. But at the same time, a good parent is not one who slavishly adheres to their child's every wish regardless of consequences either. A good parent/guardian, as we generally understand it, is one who exercises their superior experience and knowledge to make certain important decisions for a child that they are not able to make for themselves. For example, when you were a kid you may not have fully appreciated the laws of gravity, but your parent or guardian probably had a better sense of what 9.8 meters per second squared of acceleration would do to your bones when they hit the pavement and that's why you weren't allowed to play on the roof.

Good parenting or guardianship implies caring for the overall well-being of the child in one's care. But it certainly does not mean that you are obligated to ignore the big picture and sacrifice all of your deepest held values if any of them are found to be in conflict with their short-term happiness.

I have no human children of my own, but I worked as a daycare teacher for a year. One time I made the mistake of letting a couple of the little boys use the bathroom on their own. "Go right in there, do your business, and come right out," I told them. And of course they didn't. A few minutes later, when I went in to investigate, I found, to my horror, two two-and-a-half year old boys standing side by side in front of the face-high (to them) urinals, lapping up the contents like little dogs drinking water from a dish and laughing hysterically. They were obviously completely unable to understand how unsanitary, and moreover, utterly disgusting their little game truly was, and in their ignorance, they certainly seemed to be enjoying themselves. Yet I did not feel obligated to allow them to continue on those grounds.

As a teacher responsible for very young children, I felt it was only appropriate to exercise my better judgment and impose a very strict "no more drinking out of the big fountains in the bathroom" rule, even if they were unable to grasp my logic and, from their perspective, all I seemed to be doing was ruining their fun.

I always wonder how some people can be so concerned about the supposed "cruelty" of depriving cats and dogs of meat, while at the same time finding it so easy to dismiss the extreme suffering that is experienced by the animals that are made into meat cat and dog foods. Even assuming there is some small loss from the cat or dog's perspective in terms of enjoyment at mealtimes (which is certainly debatable even in itself), how can this even compare to the unbelievable cruelty of factory farming and animal slaughter?

"Does eating too much fiber make their asses hurt?" I was once asked by someone skeptical about feeding cats a vegan diet. And then, citing precedent: "Because I know that when I eat too much fiber, after a while my ass starts to ache."

"Now I'm not entirely convinced that twenty chickens," he continued, twenty being a number he pulled out of his (aching) ass to represent the number a cat eats over a lifetime, "dying relatively quickly and painlessly [a strangely casual dismissal of the plight of factory farmed chickens coming from a vegan activist] is really worse than one cat having to live, day in and day out, with a painful ass." Even as the words were leaving his lips, I was envisioning them in print. I just don't think it would be possible to come up with an example of my own that more perfectly captures the underlying ridiculousness of this line of argument than the profoundly stupid aching ass equation. Somehow I managed to come up with something semi-intelligent as a response:

"There is no reason to believe that eating vegetables causes their asses to ache. I've had vegan cats for years, and I have never been able to discern any kind of rectal discomfort in any of them. But even if we were to grant your premise, think of it this way: suppose it were twenty cats that had to die—and not just die, but spend their lives crushed into tiny, filthy cages with a number of other cats, in a constant state of pain and terror, never able to exercise even their most basic instincts, prior to that death—in order to save one chicken from a life of lying in sunbeams, rolling in catnip, getting scratched behind the ears (or whatever the chicken equivalent of a life of luxury may be) while having to endure a slightly uncomfortable ass? Would we accept the misery and death of this many cats as a necessary evil to spare one chicken from minor discomfort?

In an article called *Vegetarian Cats and Dogs: On Feeding Our Pals*, Ingrid Newkirk told about her experience encountering crates of chickens that had been abandoned outside of a slaughterhouse when the afternoon shift had left for the day:

> "Most were dead of heat prostration, but some were not. Packed in plastic crates too shallow to allow them to stand erect, the barely living chickens gasped for air, beaks open and dry, nostrils caked with dried mucus. They tried to drink melting ice from my cupped hand, but their heads were too heavy for them to hold upright.
>
> "The animals I have described are among the millions relegated to the back of the slaughter lines. They are doomed to life without painkillers, veterinary treatment, anesthesia, or even a drink of water, sometimes for several days, sometimes in extreme heat or sub-zero temperatures, often without shade or shelter, until the Agriculture Department inspec-

tor arrives to tag them 'Not Fit for Human Consumption'.

"Those who die waiting will be ground up for garden fertilizer. Those who do not will be slaughtered for 'pet' food. Old cows transformed into 'New Friskies', broken and gangrenous bones mashed into slick, green cans of 'Super Dinner'.

"Each time we go to the market, we vote with our consumer dollars. Many of us stopped voting at the butcher's counter long ago. But many of us also have animal refugees at home who still live at the expense of *those animals who suffer most*." (Italics mine.)

I have heard so many people defend their decision to feed meat to their cats and dogs by claiming that they feel it is wrong to "force their morality" onto them by making them into vegetarians. But how can this possibly be worse than inflicting the kind of immorality described above onto countless other animals instead?

Many years ago, when I was working at a veterinary hospital, there was a (dare I say?) crazy lady who used to admit her poor little kitty every couple of weeks even though there was always absolutely nothing wrong with him. "What are his symptoms, Mrs. Crazy?" we'd ask (name changed to protect the crazy). "Well," she'd tell us, "when I was holding him earlier, I pointed him in the direction of the clinic, and he meowed." As many times as he was given a clean bill of health after these episodes, she could never be convinced that when he meowed while pointed towards the clinic it possibly meant anything other than that he was sick and was requesting to be hospitalized. As a young kitten, he had once been exploring in a cupboard and apparently knocked a single loaf bread pan onto the floor. Since then, she'd been making him use it as a litter box, again unable to conceive of any reason that he might have knocked it over other than attempting to communicate to her that he wanted to pee-peepoopoo in it for perpetuity. If that seems absurd, it is only because we are able to recognize that there is a limit to our cats and dogs' ability to comprehend and communicate. Things such as when it is time to go to the vet, or which litter box is most appropriate, are our decisions, not theirs; this is not because we are "forcing" anything on them, but because it is an inherent part of our relationship. Why would food be any different?

We set up a false dichotomy when we assume that our choice is between "forcing our morality" (giving them vege-tarian food) and "honoring their choice" (giving them meat). When, exactly, did they make this choice and communicate it to us? And even if we do legitimately perceive a taste pref-erence, why would we consider that to be an unbreakable directive? If they are completely unable to understand that animals have to suffer and die in order for them to be able to eat meat then maybe they don't have enough information to make the best choice about what they should be eating.

It is difficult to imagine how some people can see them-selves as so supremely important that their enjoyment of a certain flavor takes precedence over the life-or-death concerns of everyone else. "I can't give up meat. I like it too much" is an incredibly selfish position (sociopathic, practically). So I really don't understand why so many people are so quick to attribute, by default, this same viewpoint to their own cats and dogs. Why give them so little credit? My four cats may not be able to intellectually grasp the implications of eating the bodies of other animals, but it is very clear from their interactions with me and each other that their ability to love surpasses that of any person I have ever met. So who's to say that, if they could really be made to understand the implications of eating meat, they wouldn't be appalled at the thought of it? If we're going to make assumptions, why stop at "if my cat could talk, I'm sure he'd ask for meat"? How about "if my cat were capable of speech *and empathy*, I'm sure he'd demand vegan food"?

To overrule a dietary preference that is based on an extremely limited understanding of the issues (even assuming their preference for meat is genuine in the first place) and instead select a food for them that is more in alignment with what you, their guardian, knows to be ethical is not "forcing" anything on them any more than parents of human children routinely "force" them to do such things as brush their teeth, or to not play in traffic, or to eat their vegetables, or to stay away from strangers. Our cats and dogs can make many decisions for themselves: things like whether they prefer to spend the day sitting in the window watching birds or on top of the computer sleeping, and we would be wrong to restrict their autonomy in these areas. But to make a choice as complex as which food to buy, an issue that carries ethical concerns that they couldn't possibly begin to understand, is one of our jobs. Not only is this kind of thing not contradictory to good parenting, it is an inherent part of it!

Consider a hypothetical parent or guardian of a human baby. Although she is an ethical vegan herself, she brings her child to McDonald's three meals a day. "I am able to understand the issues and have made my own choice to be a vegetarian," she reasons, "but I don't want to *force my morality* onto my daughter. She is incapable of grasping the animal suffering inherent in the production of meat and she likes the taste of hamburgers. Therefore, I am ethically bound to buy her nothing but Happy Meals."

Does this sound logical? We can't possibly believe that a young child's amorality (lack of moral reasoning ability) is not only a justification of, but actually a mandate for, our own immorality (making the voluntary choice to spend our own consumer dollars in such a way that perpetuates practices that we know to be cruel). So why would it make any more sense to apply the same reasoning to our cats and dogs?

"It Ain't Naturel."

In the previous section, I attempted to draw a parallel between our cats and dogs and human children and suggest that the decisions we make for each should be based on the same underlying factors. However, while our relationship with each is similar, their biology obviously is not. My favorite phrasing of another common objection that I often used to hear along these lines is one that I got in an email once, it's illiteracy appropriately mirroring its underlying illogic: "How can you tell people that cats and dogs should be vegan? *It ain't naturel.*"

There are so many possible angles from which to attack this issue of what is and ain't naturel (or, as those with a fifth grade education and/or spellchecker on our computer call it, "natural") that it is hard to know where to begin. I guess if I were to sum it up in a single sentence, I would have to say that it ain't as unnatural as you might think, what you're feeding your cats and dogs now probably ain't natural either, and who cares if it ain't natural anyway? I'll elaborate:

Dogs are members of the order Carnivora, but don't let the name fool you, so are giant pandas and all they eat is bamboo. Dogs are not strict carnivores; rather, they are omnivorous generalists much like ourselves, which means that their bodies are perfectly well designed to derive nutrition from a variety of sources, both plant and animal. From the Purina website:

> "The important thing about protein is that it meets the dog's nutritional needs. Contrary to what many people believe, meat protein in dog food is not inherently superior to plant protein. Like humans, dogs evolved as omnivores, able to process both plant and animal protein, and wild dogs are known to supplement their meat diet with plants. While your dog might prefer the rich, fatty taste of meat, you can keep him nutritionally fit just as easily with any high-quality plant-based dog food."

Purina! One of the largest manufacturers of meat dog food in the world!

Cats, I have to admit, are a little different. They are descended from animals that were almost entirely carnivorous, and they are designed by nature to consume flesh. If you want to tell me that a vegan diet ain't natural for cats, I am willing to concede the point—no, it sure ain't—but that brings us neatly around to point number two: what you're feeding your cat now probably isn't strictly speaking all that natural either.

Let's think about which foods animals, in a stereotypical, Tom-and-Jerry-ish sense, are generally thought to eat. Mice go crazy for wedge-shaped pieces of Swiss cheese. Dogs like rib eye steaks and chains of sausage links. For cats, three things immediately jump to mind: mice, fish (if not gold swimming in a bowl, then dead tuna on a plate with an X for an eye), and saucers of milk. Let's examine these one by one.

Saucers of milk.

Did you happen to catch comedian/professional weird guy Tom Green sucking milk directly out of a cow's udder on TV a few years back? The reaction he was going for (and the one he got) was shock, disgust, and a kind of fascinated paralysis that makes looking away or changing the channel impossible. Although most of his audience consumes dairy products on a regular basis themselves, the visual of a grown man down on his hands and knees drinking the mammary secretions of another animal, *straight out of the tap*, struck them as bizarre and incongruous. It is, of course, absurd to suppose that the health of adults of our species would depend upon the milk intended for the babies of another; the only thing that allows this belief to persist is the fact that people usually don't think about it in those terms.

Gulls and petrels drink elephant seal milk. But, other than that, I don't know of any other adult animals that drink milk of any kind, much less that of another species. Simply visualizing what a cat would look like hanging Tom Green-style off of a cow's udder is sufficient to illustrate just how natural cow's milk really is as a food for cats. A large number of them also happen to be lactose intolerant.

Fish. Especially tuna.

Try this experiment: skip your cat's breakfast one morning and bring him or her to the beach instead. Driven by hunger, what natural instincts might kick in? What are the chances that your cat will splash into the water, swim fifty or so miles out to the deep ocean, and there engage a 1200-pound animal (an adult tuna can be as large as a horse) in an underwater battle to the death in order to fulfill the natural feline diet of fish?

The idea that fish is a natural food for cats is absurd. Cats are descended from desert creatures, and they are a notoriously hydrophobic species (ever given your cat a bath?). When would they ever come across a fish, much less a gigantic deep ocean fish, in nature? Furthermore, a diet containing fish has been linked to vitamin K deficiency in cats, which can contribute to internal hemorrhages and death. From that standpoint alone they should not be eating them.

When we talk about what is natural for a cat to eat, it is obvious that it must be something that is conceivable for them, in a purely natural state, to obtain. Clearly, cow's milk and fish do not meet this standard. So how can it be that so many people misconceive of these things as being a natural part of their diet? When most people talk about what is "natural", they must not be envisioning the opportunities available to an ancestral cat living in the desert at all, but instead thinking of their own domestic cats, or cats they have seen on TV commercials. They are not thinking about what is truly natural, but only of which flavors they have been conditioned throughout life—and through meat industry pet food companies' ad campaigns—to believe that it is normal for cats to like. Of course, the fact is that many cats *do* like cow's milk and fish. The lesson to be learned from this, however, is not that these things are therefore natural, but the fact that *cats are perfectly capable of thoroughly enjoying meals that aren't.*

Mice.

Now this is a little different. We actually can envision a wild cat killing and eating a mouse, and many of us are a little bit more intimately familiar than we'd like to be with not-so-wild cats doing the same thing. Mice are small, relatively easy to catch, and they actually live in the desert. It all seems to add up, and there is good reason for that: eating live mice (and birds and insects) is what cats, in nature, would in fact do.

But here's the point: Friskies doesn't make a "Live Rodent, Bird and Insect" formulation. They rely exclusively on types of meat (cow, chicken, pig) that are, from a cat's perspective, completely foreign food sources. Unlike dogs, cats are not scavengers; they are hunters. Can you picture a cat, in nature, hunting down and killing a cow? A pig? A turkey and giblets? A "mixed grill" (whatever the hell that is)?

Many people's path to vegetarianism involves first cutting out "red meat" and then slowly phasing out "white meat" as well. I have always thought this was very strange. If one is ethically motivated, why would one cut out the large animals first? Chickens (the primary provider of "white meat") are so much smaller than cows and pigs that many more must be killed in order to obtain the same amount of meat; therefore, this common first step actually increases the amount of suffering for which one is responsible. PETA one ran a tongue-in-cheek campaign promoting the consumption of whale meat to illustrate just this same point.

Differentiating between red and white meat may be somewhat arbitrary from an ethical perspective, but it at least brings up one good point: "meat" is not one uniform substance out of which all animals are made. Fish meat, chicken meat, mouse meat, beetle meat, cow meat, and soylent green all have nutritional properties that are unique from one another, as do the different meats derived from the various parts of a given animal: muscle meat vs. organ meat, e.g.

To use an example with which most people are likely to be familiar, it is well known that fish is a good source of the omega-3 fatty acids that appear to have certain cardiovascular benefits for humans. Yet if we were to attempt to design a non-fish diet for humans that mimicked as closely as possible the nutritional properties of fish, simply substituting another "meat"—cow, chicken, pig, etc.—would be completely inadequate. None of these other "meats" happens to contain the nutrients we're after. In this case, it is only by utilizing plants (e.g., flax seeds) instead that we can hope to come close to a heart-healthy, non-fish but fish-like diet for humans.

It is similarly unwise to assume that cow or chicken meat is automatically going to be a better substitute for mouse or insect meat than a well-formulated vegetable based meal.

The motto of the Evolution company[28] is "Science Improving Nature", and, to a certain point, I think this is apt. I would not argue that nature was improved when animals were domesticated, but that happened many thousands of years ago and I don't think we can blame the Evolution company for it. I also would not promote the viewpoint that we should go to India and "improve nature" by turning all of the tigers into vegans, but what sane person would? For better or for worse, the situation we have inherited is one in which large numbers of domesticated animals—dogs and cats, but also cows, pigs and chickens—are entirely dependent upon us for their well-being. Without human ingenuity, it would be completely impossible for cats to live and be healthy without eating the bodies of other animals, and we would find ourselves playing the role of grossly underqualified God, assigned to the unenviable task of choosing which of the animals that rely on us should be allowed to live at the expense of which others. The improvement over nature, therefore, is the introduction of a third option that provides a way in which none of the animals in our care have to die.

---

28 Canada-based manufacturer of vegan cat and dog food

Although strictly speaking "unnatural" in some sense, feeding our cats and dogs a cruelty-free diet just doesn't strike me as overly offensive given the context of the regrettable situation that has been handed to us.

Government regulations regarding the human meat supply are minimal and, even at that, under-enforced. As low as the standards are, inspectors only remove a fraction of the carcasses that do not meet them. John Robbins, in *The Food Revolution*, quotes a former USDA microbiologist as saying that the chicken that finds its way onto our dinner plates is "no different than if you stuck it in the toilet and ate it."

What's truly alarming about the "pet" food industry is that it is much, much worse. The meat utilized by the "pet" food companies goes far beyond mere toilet-bowl levels of bacterial contamination. It is the stuff that, for whatever reason, cannot be sold as human food. It is so bad, it can't be put into hot dogs. It's can't be given to prisoners. *It can't even be served in the cafeteria of an elementary school!* The Not-Fit-for-Human-Consumption meats the "pet" food industry uses include animals that are so obviously diseased (visible cancerous tumors, e.g.) that even the understaffed, overworked USDA inspectors were able to pick them off the line. These are the "downer" animals that Ingrid Newkirk encountered outside of the slaughterhouse. These are supermarket meats that have passed their expiration date, or meats that have become spoiled when a refrigeration unit has broken. This is what we feed to our cats and dogs.

When a can of cat or dog food includes "meat" on its lists of ingredients, you know that there are some body parts from some mammal contained within, but there are no regulations beyond that. "Meat" doesn't mean Filet Mignon, it doesn't mean top sirloin, and it doesn't even mean hamburger. It doesn't mean muscle tissue, or nutrient-dense organ meat. It doesn't mean that it has passed any sort of inspection, or that it necessarily has any nutritional value whatsoever. It means, simply, some part of some mammal. "Meat" can be blood, bone or brain tissue. "Meat" can be roadkill. The fur and skeleton of an opossum that was scraped off the highway, for example, are "meat". "Meat" can even be cats and dogs.

It is standard industry practice to make cat and dog food out of the bodies of cats and dogs. Five million or so cats and dogs are euthanized in shelters each year; where do you suppose they go? There's no graveyard for unadopted animals, and we sure as hell know that their kind isn't welcome over at Rainbow Bridge. The shelters have a disposal problem, and the "pet" food industry has a desire to use the cheapest meat possible and is conveniently devoid of ethics or quality standards.

In a visceral sense, most people find the practice of using the bodies of cats and dogs in cat and dog food to be the most abhorrent of the meat industry's transgressions against nature. Forced cannibalism almost seems sadistic. But in terms of what is really unnatural, it isn't even close. I mentioned that spoiled supermarket meats find their way into cat and dog food, but what I didn't mention is that they are not required to take them out of the Styrofoam packaging first. I mentioned downer animals, but didn't mention that they consider it a waste of effort to remove ear tags. I mentioned cats and dogs, but didn't mention that flea collars are not routinely removed, and that sodium pentobarbital—the injectable euthanasia solution that is commonly used[29]—remains in the finished product in measurable quantities[30]. I will discuss health concerns in a later section, but this one is a no-brainer: are Styrofoam, plastic, flea collars, and an injectable poison—one that is considered "humane" because it is so toxic that even a tiny quantity kills instantly—part of the natural, healthy diet of our dogs and cats?

Which represents the greater crime against nature: providing cats and dogs with a vegetarian diet that is specially formulated to meet their nutritional needs, or giving them a highly-processed meat-based food consisting of feathers, tumors, nerve tissue, cat and dog carcasses, ground-up plastic and a poison specifically designed to kill them?

The most "natural" food that our cats could get is if they were allowed to hunt for themselves, and many people argue in favor of allowing them to roam freely outdoors on these grounds. The part of the equation that they are missing, however, is the fact that this is only "natural" from the standpoint of the cat. Although some are likely to have snuck aboard ships here and there before then, cats were only deliberately brought to the United States from England in order to control the rat population in 1749. In other words, they are a relatively new arrival against which prey

---

29 not to be confused with sodium pentathol, which only makes cats and dogs tell the truth
30 an FDA study conducted in 1998 found sodium pentobarbital in 41 different brands of meat-based dog foods

species are not equipped to adequately defend themselves; it is "natural" for cats to eat small mammals, but it is not at all "natural" for small North American rodents to have to deal with cats.

Unlike other natural predators, who evolve symbiotically with their prey to the ultimate benefit of both, cats have another unfair advantage: us. By taking care of them (giving them shots, offering them shelter, etc.) we give them a competitive advantage that no other species of natural predator has ever experienced. As a result, it is not even a contest; cats have the potential to absolutely devastate local songbird and rodent populations. In fact, cats are often thought to be the species that is directly responsible for the second-most extinction events worldwide (guess who's number one).

Another diet that some people employ in an attempt to simulate what is most "natural" for cats and dogs to be eating is the deliciously named BARF diet (which stands for Bones And Raw Food). This runs against some of the same difficulties as other meat-based diets. Raw or cooked, it is simply not natural for dogs and cats to be eating cows and chickens. And here again, while eating their meat raw may be a step closer to what cats and dogs would be doing in nature, forcing the animals out of which the BARF is made to die in a slaughterhouse, regardless of whether their flesh is ultimately cooked before being served, is hardly respectful of what is natural for them.

Over the years, I have met many, many people who tell me that they do not give their cats and dogs a vegetarian diet, but then proudly go on to say that they give them raw meat, or feed them a "premium" food, as if they've struck some kind of middle ground and expect me to approve of their choice. Quite the contrary, when you really think about it: whereas the low-priced supermarket brands are atrocious, they contribute to the profitability of animal slaughter less so than the more expensive brands. Using dogs and cats as a source of meat is morally disturbing, but at least doing so doesn't drive an industry (in other words, the shelters are not being paid, and they don't kill more cats and dogs just to meet the industry's demand for cheap meat). When you buy a "premium" brand or high-quality cut of raw meat, you are no longer increasing the profitability of animal slaughter by creating a market for its waste materials; you are now increasing the market for its main products, giving even more money to the industry, and directly mandating the slaughter of even more animals. This hardly seems like an adequate solution for an ethical vegan who is serious about reducing animal suffering.

Point number three: *who cares what's natural?*

When you really think about it, this "it ain't naturel" argument is a cop-out. There is nothing in the least bit natural about our relationship with domesticated animals at all. There is nowhere "in nature" that one animal lives entirely at the expense of the other. We give our cats and dogs shots to protect them against diseases (is vaccination "natural"?), microchip them in case they get lost (simulating the tracking database that cats, "in nature", refer to when they can't find their way home?), surgically manipulate their ability to reproduce, let them live, rent-free, in our homes, for Christ's sake. So why only when it comes to the substance of their diet (because we certainly don't insist that they go about obtaining their food in a natural way either), do we find ourselves so rigidly bound to adhere to what we perceive to be natural (and never mind that our perception is completely wrong)? By what logic is that one area of our lives, and this one area alone, dictatorially governed by nature while we have the ability to use our better judgment and technology to make improvements upon every single other aspect of their existence?

What is natural has never been the basis for what is moral. Our whole animal rights movement is not based on what is natural (because, like it or not, it is perfectly natural for humans to eat meat and for the weaker to be dominated by the stronger), but on what is ethical; what *should be* rather than what has *historically been.*

As vegan activists, one of our common frustrations is dealing with people who use circular reasoning to justify the status quo based on the fact that it is the status quo—"people have always eaten meat"; "if eating meat were so terrible, then why does almost everyone do it?" This is anti-progressive, backwards thinking. Yet it is exactly the reasoning vegans often use to justify feeding their cats and dogs meat: cats and dogs have always eaten meat, and most of them still eat meat today; therefore it must be ethically justifiable to continue feeding them meat. And on the contrary, it is unethical to upset the status quo by attempting to feed them in a way that doesn't directly cause the suffering and death of other animals.

Does that seem like the way a vegan should think?

One of my favorite anti-vegan quotes is an angry comment that was hurled at me at a demo outside of a McDonald's many years ago: "*We've been eating meat for hundreds of years.*" And, comical time scale errors aside, the guy isn't wrong. My answer, and probably yours, is *so what?* We've had war, slavery, racism, genocide, oppression of women and all kinds of other terrible things for "hundreds" of years too. Does that ethically justify continuing these things as well?

> "Cats do not require ingredients, they require the nutrients those ingredients provide. Corn [for example] provides a number of nutrients required by cats, including protein, carbohydrates, vitamins and minerals. In addition, the vegetable oil found naturally in corn is an important source of linoleic acid, a fatty acid that is essential for cats of all ages.
>
> "...Cats are carnivores. [But] keep in mind, a protein molecule is made up of a combination of amino acids. The way amino acids are arranged determines the nature of the protein. Whether protein is obtained from plants or animals is not as critical as the balance of amino acids. There are 23 different amino acids. Ten are considered essential to a dog's diet because the system of the cat and dog cannot manufacture

these amino acids in large enough quantities to maintain body functions. Animal products are excellent sources of protein, but plants also contain valuable amino acids. *Plant proteins, when combined with* animal proteins or *other plant proteins, can provide the proper amino acid balance for every life stage of the cat and dog.*"

I added the italics for emphasis: "Plant proteins, when combined with... other plant proteins, can provide the proper amino acid balance for every life stage of the cat and dog." Once again, this is not a quote from some extremist animal rights group pushing a radical agenda, but from Purina, one of the largest players in the meat "pet" food industry. It almost strikes me as bizarre that they would admit this, when so many vegans will not!

"A man can live and be healthy without killing animals for food; therefore, if he eats meat, he participates in taking animal life merely for the sake of his appetite. And to act so is immoral." This was not said by Purina; it is from Tolstoy. Tweaked slightly, but still retaining the same essential meaning, this becomes:

"A cat or dog can live and be healthy without having animals killed for food; therefore, if we give them meat, we participate in taking animal life merely for the sake of their appetite.

"*And to act so is immoral.*"

Pop Rocks & Coke

Vegan activists sometimes try to win converts by distributing lists of world-class vegetarian athletes, but have you ever considered what a list of *meat-eating* athletes would look like? At the close of the 20th century, ESPN released a list of the top 100 athletes of the previous 100 years. Of these, only #19, Martina Navratilova, is a confirmed vegetarian. About four others are sometimes listed as vegetarian, but I'm a little skeptical (if Hank Aaron was a strict vegetarian during his playing career, for example, then I will go to the Hall of Fame and eat his hat). And the other three: #35 Secretariat, #84 Citation, and #97 Man o' War, were horses. At the very least, then, the top 100 athletes include 92 who ate meat: Michael Jordan, Babe Ruth, Muhammad Ali, Jim Brown, Wayne Gretzky and Jesse Owens, to name just a few.

When I first became vegetarian, I believed that I would be in some way doing myself harm. I had been brought up with very conventional views of nutrition and human health, and really believed that by eliminating meat from my diet I was swearing off a full 25% of the food groups that were necessary for proper nutrition. I just didn't care. To some extent, this was probably because at the time I was a teenager and pretty much thought that I was bulletproof anyway. But beyond that, it's because my health just wasn't really the issue. I became vegetarian because it was the morally right thing to do, not because I thought it would protect me from certain diseases or extend my lifespan.

When, years later, I found out that there are very good reasons to believe that vegetarianism is not only adequate but actually *healthier* than a diet that includes meat, I was pleasantly surprised and maybe a little relieved. But it was not, and is still not, necessary that this be the case. If new studies reveal tomorrow that the four food groups were dead-on accurate after all and that 2-3 servings of meat per day really are necessary to maintain maximum health, I'll be disappointed. But I'll still be vegan.

We often talk about the three main pillars to the vegan/vegetarian message: health, environment, and concern for animals, that are emphasized by various animal rights/vegetarian organizations in differing proportions and in different ways. Most probably use all of these arguments from time to time, attempting to tailor their message to fit whatever their particular audience happens to be at the time.

I think that this kind of diversity in our message is great; the preponderance of evidence that points to the superiority of a vegan diet is quite astounding. The only problem is that I think we sometimes make the mistake of overselling our case; we do not argue that, all things considered, veganism is the best choice; we instead tend to argue that veganism is *always* the best choice in *every* circumstance and for every reason. The effect of doing this, unfortunately, may be the opposite of what we intend: instead of viewing us as intelligent people who have chosen veganism for logical, reasonable reasons, many skeptics instead conclude that we are blind dogmatists pushing an agenda. Sometimes we are so successful at making veganism sound good that we accidentally make it sound too good to be true.

The vegetarian athletes list may or may not be a perfect example. If we try to present our little list (Martina, some unsubstantiated rumors, and a bunch of people you've never heard of) as irrefutable evidence that following a vegetarian diet enhances sports performance, then we look ridiculous. John Salley is a prominent vegetarian who won four NBA championships—something many vegans are inclined to point to proudly. On the other hand, Steve Kerr won four championships as well... and he's a 6'1" white guy. Thus it is precisely as valid to claim that vegetarianism gives one an edge on the basketball court as it is to argue that short whiteness does; as a 6'1" white vegan myself, I can only express my regret that none of these characteristics really seems to provide much of an advantage. I would never say that Michael Jordan was a better player because of his meat consumption, but at the same time it is really hard to make the claim that his performance was impeded by it. But does it really have to have been? Does meat have to make you a bad basketball player in order for us to conclude that we shouldn't eat it?

There is definitely potential value in our list of vegetarian athletes, but only if we are using it to make a much more modest point: that it is *possible* to be an elite athlete while not eating meat. Suddenly it doesn't matter that the vast majority of Olympic gold medalists, Heisman Trophy winners, and champions of your local bowling league have all eaten meat; we're not disputing that. We're no longer saying that being vegetarian *increases* your chances of achieving these things; we're simply pointing out that it doesn't *decrease* your odds. Phrased this way, our argument no longer provides an additional—likely disingenuous—reason why veganism is *better*, yet it now much more effectively refutes, *in a way that is highly reasonable and difficult to dismiss*, the common assumption that veganism and sports inherently don't mix. Once that excuse ("I have to eat meat; I'm an athlete") is out of the way, we can talk about some of the many other reasons why veganism really is superior (animal suffering, environmental, etc.) that actually *can* be backed up with verifiable facts. The credibility we gain by not overstating our claim when the issue is athletic performance makes it more likely that people will take us seriously when we make our other, more reasonable, arguments.

Of the three pillars, I find health to be the weakest for a couple of reasons. First of all, look around you; does it look like anyone gives a damn about what foods are the healthiest? Two-thirds of Americans are overweight and yet they continue to stuff their fat little faces with French fries and doughnuts. They don't do this due to a mistaken perception that these are nutritious, but simply because they are weak-willed and rationalize the continuation of habits that they know to be unhealthy.

Secondly, this is the argument that is potentially the most subject to reversal. Alcohol, for example, was considered to be very detrimental to health for centuries, and yet we now know that it is actually as good for the heart as it is for the soul. What if the same thing were to happen with meat, or eggs? What happens if a pharmaceutical company perfects a pill that allows you to eat as much fat and cholesterol as you want without negative consequences? What if genetic engineering creates chickens with the nutritional properties of a stalk of broccoli?

Judicious use of health statistics can definitely be valu-able in making our case, but again, I think we need to be careful not to oversell. It is not *necessary* for veganism to lower heart disease and cancer rates in order to conclude that it is the best choice; if it does, that is just an added bonus. All that is actually *necessary* is that it is not devastat-ing to one's personal health. We need to reassure people that they can still get plenty of protein and calcium without eating animal products; we don't need to tell them that they will become immortal and break the world's record in the hammer throw.

James Peden, who, in the late 1980's, developed Veg-ecat—the world's first 100% vegan, 100% nutritionally complete cat food—makes it very clear in his (regrettably, now out of print) book *Vegetarian Cats and Dogs*, that his primary goal was never to create health food for dogs and cats. He was simply trying to design a cruelty-free option that was nutritionally adequate, one that would allow the cats and dogs who ate it to be more or less as healthy as their meat-eating counterparts. "Along the way," he says, "we had a pleasant surprise: fed properly, vegetarian pets can look forward to being healthier." The Evolution company makes similar claims about increased life expectancy and freedom from certain diseases.

I do not find it necessary to echo the claims of the Vegepet and Evolution companies that cats and dogs being fed a vegetarian diet will necessarily be healthier than those who are fed meat. Although, over the years, I received positive feedback from literally hundreds of vegancats.com's many thousands of regular customers, I simply don't have the data to *prove* that vegan food is the healthiest of all options. *More to the point, I will not argue that veganism is the absolute healthiest diet for cats and dogs because whether it is or is not is simply not morally relevant.*

I have said that I would remain vegan myself even if I were to find out that it were not the absolute best choice from the standpoint of my personal health. If it meant that my lifespan would be a little shorter, or my bones a little more brittle, I'd gladly trade these things in exchange for alleviating the suffering of animals. But what if remaining vegan meant that I'd drop dead tomorrow? We hear these kind of hypotheticals from meat-eaters all the time: what if a cattle rancher handed me a gun and told me he'd set two cows free if I shot myself in the head? Would I do it? Theoretically, it sounds like a pretty good two-for-one trade, but I don't know if I'm that big of a person. (Actually, I've thought about this quite a bit, and I know exactly what I'd do if I ever found myself in this situation... I'd shoot *him* in the kneecap and ride the cows down to Mexico.)

When I became vegan myself, I didn't require a scientific study to prove that it was the healthiest choice possible. But honestly, I think I might have second thoughts if I were convinced that being vegan meant choosing immediate, fatal organ failure. In other words, I didn't need proof that I would be the absolute healthiest person in the history of the world before I would stop killing animals and eating them, but I suppose that I do like to have the assurance that I can be reasonably healthy or at least roughly as healthy as I would be otherwise.

Fortunately, just by looking at the vegans around me gives me all of the evidence I need to be at ease with my choice: there are lots of them, and most of them seem to live perfectly normal lives without developing mysterious diseases and dropping dead all around me. Are they the very healthiest people that have ever existed? I don't know, and I don't care. If their health is diminished at all-- *"if"*-- then it is such a tiny amount that I can't even perceive it. Compared to the amount of suffering their choice is sparing, it is nothing.

Unfortunately, when it comes to vegetarian cat and dog food, what many people seem to be asking for is not *adequacy*, but *irrefutable proof of superiority*. Sometimes I think that this is because they are so used to the idea that veganism, in humans, is both the most ethical and the healthiest that they subconsciously blur the line between the two. *If it is really the most ethical*, they say, *then prove that it is the healthiest*. More often, though, I think it is just that they love their cats and dogs so much that they temporarily forget to care about everyone else. They are so focused on what they perceive to be in the best interests of their own dogs and cats that they forget the other side of the equation: the "food" animals whose lives are in their hands.

There are also many people who would be satisfied with the simple assurance that vegan cats and dogs can be more or less as healthy as meat-eaters, but aren't convinced that they have even that. Some people actually believe that by switching their cats and dogs to a cruelty-free diet, they might be doing them great, irreparable harm—killing them even. It is certainly understandable why this fear would cause hesitation.

I used to get letters from customers all the time whose pets' health had visibly improved once the switch was made; often skin and digestive problems had gone away (probably because these are often caused by an allergy to meat by-products), and they reported higher energy levels and the resumption of kittenish/puppyish behavior that hadn't been seen in years. But every once in a while I also used to get a letter from someone whose cat had died (or more often someone whose friend knows someone whose cat had died) while being fed a vegan diet. Every once in a while these stories began to circulate and scare people. You may have heard of some of these, and they might have scared you too.

Unlike most people, as will become immediately apparent, whenever I heard a story like this, I always made it my business to follow up and get to the bottom of the matter. And I have to admit, what I found out is scary as hell. It's scary how readily people will believe and spread a rumor that has such immense consequences for the well-being of animals without even bothering to verify the facts.

One example: a few years ago, there was an email going around that stated that vegan cat food had been proven to cause horrible fatal diseases in cats. If you have been giving your cat vegan food for more than 6 months, it said, you must go get a blood test IMMEDIATELY. Two contact numbers were given for questions and further information. One was an "expert" on the subject, and the other a veterinarian from the Animal Protection Institute. I called the "expert" first.

Remember that old, old TV commercial for... something... in which the first person phones two friends about... something... and then they tell two friends, and then they tell two friends, and then THEY tell two friends? Pretty soon the screen is filled with teeny, tiny pictures of all the friends that have been called. That's an example of exponential growth. Now think about how long it takes to phone two friends compared to how long it takes just to forward an email that seems important to your entire mailing list. You forward to your mailing list, and then they forward to their mailing list, and then THEY forward to THEIR mailing list. Now you might not know Kevin Bacon, and you might not know anybody that knows him, but you can bet that in about three hours, your forwarded letter is sitting in his inbox.

Seriously, I have no idea how many people might have gotten this same letter about the perils of vegan cat food before I did, but, the way animal rights people are with their mailing lists, it could easily have been thousands if not tens of thousands. I have no way of knowing how many of these people accepted it, rejected it, or deleted it without reading, but I do know that out of all of these people, I was the very first to call for more information. I found this out because when I began asking the "expert" questions, she stopped me and told me that she had no idea what the hell I was talking about.

"You were listed as a contact person about diseases caused by vegan cat food..."

"I WAS? I have no idea what that might be about..."

I verified her name and phone number, but she still didn't have a clue.

"Sorry to bother you then," I said. "The email also lists a vet from API as a contact, so I guess I'll just call her and hope that she knows what this is all about..."

Sudden recognition. "OHHH!!! Wait! I'll bet I do know what this is. A few years ago, I called API and asked if they had had any reports of cats suffering from any kind of a vitamin deficiency on vegan food. I don't know why they'd list me as a contact person though..."

"Well, were you calling them because you had a cat who became sick while on a vegan diet?"

"No. Actually, I've fed my cats vegan food for years and they're all doing great. I feel totally comfortable giving it to them. I was just wondering if they'd heard anything about anyone else having problems?"

"Had they?"

"No."

This, the "expert" on fatal deficiencies caused by vegan cat food.

So, I called the vet at API. "No, I haven't heard of any reports of any deficiencies caused by vegan cat food," she said. "But I don't really know enough about it to endorse it either. Before I could unequivocally say that it provided adequate nutrition, I'd want to look at some blood tests of cats that had been vegan for at least six months." Had she ever looked at a single blood test of a vegan cat? Nope. Did she think it was vital that anyone who had a vegan cat should rush out to the vet and have him or her tested? Uh-uh.

This is how rumors start. This is how every single human on the face of the earth can tell you that Mikey "Likes It" died from mixing Pop Rocks and Coke, despite the fact that this makes absolutely no sense[31].

Another time I received a very accusatory email from a woman charging me with killing cats. She had had a vegan cat once, she informed me, and the cat had died of malnutrition. I wrote back to her, clarifying that what I was actually trying to do was pretty much the opposite—to save animals—and that I would never knowingly contribute to the death of cats. "There are thousands of cats out there

---

31 the thing that makes both of these products fizzy is the same—CO_2. And what happens when CO_2 is mixed with more CO_2 inside a human stomach? Impolite gaseous expulsion of one kind or another, certainly not a lethal explosion

who seem to do quite well on a vegan diet, and I have never heard of one dying of a deficiency before. But I would be very interested in hearing your story. Which specific nutrients had been deficient? What organs had failed? Etc." In a patronizing tone, she explained to me that her cat had died of "mal-nu-tri-tion" (a general deficiency of everything that caused everything to fail simultaneously) after eating vegan dog food for several years.

Wait... hold the phone. Vegan dog food?

Cats and dogs both live in our houses, and they're both furry, but there the similarity ends. Their nutritional needs are different. Vegan dog food is designed to supply what a dog needs, and vegan cat food is designed for cats. A dog, because their requirements are less strict, can probably be perfectly healthy eating cat food, but not so in reverse. What this woman proved—unfortunately, the hard way—is that cats can't be healthy on dog food; but she didn't prove a thing about how healthy they can be on vegan cat food.

Similarly, there was another case in which a man cited his friend's bad experience with vegan cats as a reason for his skepticism. What had the friend been feeding? Rice and vegetables, with no specially formulated vegan cat food or supplements at all. I guessed that the cat went blind and then died of an enlarged heart. Yup. Taurine deficiency.

"Of course he did," I explained. "Vegetables alone do not supply all of the nutrients that a cat needs. But it is exactly those deficiencies for which the vegan cat foods are specifically designed to compensate."

Unconvinced: "Yeah... but the cat was vegan... and he died."

Where's the logic? How can we reject out of hand a specially supplemented diet on the grounds that an *unsupplemented* diet is inadequate? Would we claim that penicillin doesn't cure syphilis on the grounds that someone who *didn't* receive treatment had succumbed to the disease?

Of course, veterinarians don't usually help to dispel the rampant misinformation much either.

Veterinary students, like their human counterparts (you know what I mean), receive disturbingly little instruction about nutrition. In keeping with the western medicine tradition, their education is mainly centered on how to cure illnesses, not on how to prevent them. Once your cat or dog has cancer, they can whip out a scalpel and excise it with incredible skill. But when it comes to common sense issues about how to prevent cancer (e.g., don't feed them a diet made from old chicken tumors and euthanasia solution) they are generally not as strong.

It is not even so much the relative lack of instruction about issues relating to diet that concerns me though. What I find truly troublesome is the source of educational materials for the precious few nutritional courses that they do take. These are written by the meat pet food companies, and consist of the results of studies that they themselves have conducted or paid to have done. Sometimes they are generous enough to actually donate a company representative to serve as the instructor of the class as well!

It is very telling that, even to this day, most doctors continue to eat the standard American diet. It's telling that, when I asked for the "vegetarian" meal during a hospital stay several years back, I was served a hot dog and a packet of Oreos[32]. I have tremendous respect for someone who can perform brain surgery or transplant an organ, when I can't even assemble a six-piece bookcase without screwing up, but I think that most of us know that doctors trained in the western tradition are not to be trusted as a source of information when it comes to nutrition. It's simply not a part of their profession. So why would we assume any different about DVMs? Their training places the same emphasis on curing, rather than preventing, disease, and what little they do learn about nutrition could not be from a more biased source. At least medical doctors do not take their nutrition courses at Hamburger U. If you ask them a question about nutrition, at least they're not looking up the answer in a reference book published by Chick-Fil-A.

Despite this limitation, most veterinarians are, at this point, willing to concede that dogs can be perfectly healthy on a vegetarian diet. Yet 9 out of 10 will still tell you that you're a goddamned lunatic if you think you can feed your cat without meat.

I had a vet tell me once that I needed to put one of my cats on a meat diet.

"Why?" I asked. "What is it that you think he's not getting?"

---

32 this, of course, was back when Oreos were still made with lard

"Well, for one thing, there is an amino acid called taurine that..."

I interrupted her, explaining where the taurine came from and mentioning that I had already had a blood test done (to settle the same debate with a different vet) which had come back with a taurine level 10 times greater than that considered to be necessary to avoid deficiency, and three times that of an average cat. Was there anything else she was concerned about?

"I don't know specifically. I just think that, in general, he'd be healthier if he got some meat in his diet."

Her objections were not based on anything she learned in vet school or had observed in cats that she had treated in practice, but on the same vague, unsupported biases that most people have. The only difference is that she was wearing a white coat.

Cats and dogs get sick occasionally. It happens. They get weird skin things. They throw up. Sometimes they even die. When they are being fed the slaughterhouse waste products sold by the companies that write the medical texts, the official cause of their ailment is often "unknown". These things happen, your vet tells you, we don't always know why. A shot of cortisone should do it. Or some antibiotics. Or temporarily switching them to one of the "Prescription"[33] diets. Yet when a vegan cat encounters the same periodic disorders,

---

33 I say "Prescription" in quotes because the fact is that no prescription is actually necessary to buy these foods. There are certain brands that you can only buy through veterinarians, but this has nothing to do with any kind of laws regulating their distribution. It is simply an extremely clever marketing ploy by the manufacturer to distribute them this way

the diet is invariably blamed, even when to do so stretches all bounds of reason: hair falling out? Must be the vegan food. Got the sniffles? Cats need meat, you know. Hit by the car? Probably not getting enough taurine! This can be very frustrating. People used to write to me all the time: my cat has X problem, and my vet says it's probably the vegan food. Over the years, I heard it blamed for almost everything once, yet, interestingly enough, very rarely twice. How strong can the link between vegan food and a given health problem really be if only one out of thousands of vegan cats are affected in that way? How can we assume cause and effect when meat-eating cats experience all of the same problems periodically as well? Many vets seem to have a bias against vegan food in general, and will use any excuse (whatever the cat happens to come into the office for next) to steer them back towards meat.

* * *

As I have said, it isn't necessary that vegetarian food be healthier than meat in order to conclude that it is the best choice. It is not necessary that meat cat and dog foods contribute to poor health and disease in the same way that consuming animal products is linked to these things in humans. Even if it were the case that meat cat and dog foods offered perfect nutrition and guaranteed a long, happy, disease-free life for any cat or dog who ate them, this would not outweigh the negatives associated with making this choice (the short, unhappy, disease-ridden lives of the animals they are eating). It is not necessary, but some days the clouds open up and the sun just seems to shine down upon you.

Whole books have been written on the subject of all the toxic, disease-causing, and just plain disgusting stuff that goes into meat cat and dog foods. The dangling-participle-ly named *Foods Pets Die For* by Ann N. Martin, for example, is little more than a 130-page list of chemicals, preservatives, hormones, pesticides, and diseased animal parts and the illnesses each one can cause. Well-known veterinarian Michael W. Fox makes a comparison between this book and Rachel Carson's *Silent Spring*, and I really don't feel like that's much of an exaggeration. The gulf between what most of us believe we are feeding to our meat-eating cats and dogs and what we are actually giving them is enormous.

"Plump whole chickens, choice cuts of beef, fresh grains, and all the wholesome nutrition your dog or cat will ever need," the API report *What's Really in Pet Food* begins. "These are the images pet food manufacturers promulgate through the media and advertising. This is what the $11 billion per year U.S. pet food industry wants consumers to believe they are buying when they purchase their products. What most consumers don't know is that the pet food industry is an extension of the human food and agriculture industries. Pet food provides a market for slaughterhouse offal, grains considered 'unfit for human consumption', and similar waste products to be turned into profit. This waste includes intestines, udders, esophagi, and possibly diseased and cancerous animal parts."

Dr. Richard H. Pitcairn, DVM, in his highly-respected *Natural Health for Cats & Dogs*, cites another DVM and former federal meat inspector, Dr. P.F. McGargle, as saying that, in his opinion, "feeding slaughterhouse wastes to animals increases their chances of getting cancer and other degenerative diseases. Those wastes, he reports, can include moldy, rancid or spoiled meats as well as tissue severely riddled with cancer."

When I worked at the vet clinic, I watched or assisted with a number of different kinds of surgeries. Mostly they were spays, neuters and declaws (which is a whole 'nother topic that goes way beyond what I'm talking about here; but, suffice it to say, there is a lot of blood, panic and discomfort that people don't necessarily see. On more than one occasion, the morning following a declaw surgery, there would be so much blood caked onto the Plexiglas window of a cage that I couldn't even see the cat inside). Every once in a while, though, a cat would come through who needed some less common, miscellaneous procedure done. This was always an exciting break from the daily routine, and you felt lucky if you got to hang out and watch the doctor cutting into some new part of a cat in some way that you'd never seen before.

One case that particularly stands out is a cat who came in for exploratory surgery; they were going to open him up, poke around a little bit, and see if they could figure out just what was wrong with him. I watched calmly as the incision was made and as the skin was pulled back to offer a good view of his insides. And then it was suddenly vividly apparent, even to me, exactly what was causing the problem: cancer. Not a few small tumors, isolated to a specific region or two, but *everywhere*. Every organ, it seemed, was overgrown with a sheath of it; every inch of intestine, which the doctor unraveled to inspect more closely, was dotted with little white cancerous growths. I had never seen anything like it. I had expected to see an abnormal organ or two, something that was not quite right, but nothing had prepared me for the sight of a living, breathing cat whose entire insides were completely rotten with disease.

That was a meat-eating cat.

Another memorable case was an extremely obese cat who came in with breathing difficulties, whose heart suddenly stopped on the examination table. With all of the doctors in the hospital working on him they managed to resuscitate him, but it was obvious that his long-term prospects were not good. His family was notified, but he arrested a second time while they were on their way. Miraculously, though, he was brought back one more time, just long enough for them to say their tearful goodbyes and hold him as he was injected with euthanasia solution. On autopsy, his chest cavity was found to be so stuffed full of fat that his heart and lungs had literally been crushed.

Another meat-eater.

In the time I worked at the vet clinic, there was not one single client, other than me, with vegetarian cats at home, and yet we were constantly inundated with seriously ill cats. Cats with urinary tract problems were among our most frequent visitors. Cats with diabetes were routine. Cancer was common. Kidney failure, even more so. Respiratory symptoms, infected gums, runny eyes, itchy skin—we saw all of these things daily. Every single one of these cats ate meat.

How can we make the mistake of assuming that by giving them meat, we are guaranteeing their health?

Martin cites a study that *proves* that eating sodium pentobarbital euthanasia solution can cause health problems in dogs, but, again, do we really need a study to tell us this? What about deoxynivalenol, which forms when grains become wet and moldy (and are deemed Unfit for Human Comsumption and made into pet food)? How much more information do we need beyond the fact that it's common name—*vomitoxin*—was cleverly created by combining the word "vomit" with the word "toxin". Take your best guess: is that a *good* thing or a *bad* thing to be feeding to our cats and dogs?

Pitcairn lists several common preservatives that meat brands use, such as propylene glycol ("known to cause illness in dogs"), propyl gallate ("suspected of causing liver damage"), BHT ("cause of liver damage, metabolic stress, fetal abnormality, and serum cholesterol increase"), sodium nitrite ("can produce powerful carcinogenic compounds") and ethoxyquin ("among the compounds most suspect as causes of severe health problems in dogs").

Cats and dogs may appreciate a bowl of green kibble for St. Patrick's Day, but the other 364 days a year you wouldn't think artificial colors would be necessary to entice them to eat a certain brand. Once again, though, we are the ones deciding which foods to purchase for them, and we tend to be plenty stupid enough to be influenced by something as ridiculous as the color of a processed food pellet. Artificial colors are therefore added to many meat foods as a matter of course, with predictable results: Pitcairn lists red no. 40 as a "possible carcinogen" and blue no. 2 as "shown in studies to increase dogs' sensitivities to fatal viruses". Others have not been studied enough to draw conclusions, but common sense tells us that, at the very least, they aren't *improving* the health of our cats and dogs.

I don't think it's necessary to belabor the point. Again, the healthfulness or non-healthfulness of meat cat and dog foods is tangential to the moral issue. The only reason I mention it at all is because I know there are people who intellectually agree with the moral point of feeding vegetarian food, but are still feeling a nagging emotional reaction: *but I could never live with myself if I did anything to damage the health of my cats and dogs.*

Then step number one should be getting them as far away from commercially produced meat "pet" foods as possible.

We can all point to a cat or dog who lived 20 happy years on cheap supermarket brand food. Many people will do just this when confronted with the kind of claims I have just mentioned: *if meat cat and dog food are really so terrible, why didn't this one get sick and die at a much younger age?*

I don't know why. Maybe it's divine intervention. Maybe it's genetics. Maybe it's luck. What do you tell people when they try to argue that meat is healthy for humans, citing their 100-year-old great uncle's lifelong diet of mutton chops and cigarettes? Maybe it's that. But it's sure as hell not because there is nothing horribly wrong with the products marketed by the meat pet food industry.

If the lifespan of cats and dogs has gone up in the past half century, it is probably because our veterinarians are so well trained in lifesaving techniques and because we have the technological and pharmaceutical ability to do things that could never have been dreamed of before. *It is not because the $11 billion per year arm of the animal slaughter industry that markets waste products as pet food has hit upon a magical formula that ensures decades of radiant health and happiness for 79 cents a can!*

We know enough to disbelieve the dairy industry when they tell us that milk is a natural or does a body good. We know that beef is not, in fact, what's for dinner. But when the meat pet food industry tells us that pelletized or canned slaughterhouse waste products, the bodies of dogs and cats, moldy grains, flea collars, euthanasia solution, hormones, chemical preservatives, pesticides, livestock antibiotics, and toxic levels of heavy metals like lead and mercury are not only adequate but actually *necessary* for proper nutrition, many of us accept this claim at face value. For many vegans, this is the last slaughterhouse industry lie to which we are still susceptible.

Cat Urine

As I mentioned at the outset, I currently have four cats—three of whom are strict vegetarians and one fat little meat-eater[34].

The oldest, Olivia, is thirteen years old and has been completely vegan (eating both Vegecat and Evolution brand foods) her entire life. Her fur is thick, shiny and beautiful, her eyes are bright, and she still retains the playfulness of a kitten. A recent blood test came back perfect: no sign of kidney or other organ deterioration, even though a slight

---

34 in the interest of full disclosure, I should mention that Frances—that cat who I likened to Gary Coleman in the first edition, due to both her congenital kidney defect and the fact her parents abandoned her—succumbed to her illness a few years back at the age of nine. While a cynic might wonder if her vegan diet accelerated the progression of her disease, others may be inclined to give it credit for her having survived an almost unprecedented three additional years after entering the "terminal" phase of kidney failure. Either interpretation would be complete conjecture—I know of no compelling reason to believe that a vegan diet is either beneficial or detrimental to a cat's kidney health

decline in functioning would be normal or even expected in a cat her age.

Sam, also thirteen, has been vegan for five years. While I probably wouldn't expect him to win any beauty contests (particularly if they award points for breath odor), he's never experienced any serious illnesses in his life either.

Gordy, ten, is shockingly large and muscular for a cat. Another lifelong vegan, he too enjoys radiant health; his teeth and coat are those of a kitten 1/10th his age. Gordy's favorite snacks include tomatoes and green peppers, and the few times he's been presented with meat in his life, he's looked upon it with the same disdain that you or I might.

And then there's Jude.

If I were in a high school debate club, and were assigned to defend the proposition that cats should not be vegan, I wouldn't waste any time on "it ain't naturel", "it's wrong to force your morality" or "where's their taurine going to come from?" All of these are ultimately flawed arguments, based on faulty premises or relying on bad reasoning. Of course, if I thought that this was a winnable argument at all, this book would have been a colossally stupid undertaking. Yet if I were forced to pick the area in which the idea of veganism in cats is most vulnerable to attack, I would concern myself with one thing and one thing only: urine.

Camels, as we all know, are notable for their ability to survive for extended periods of time in the blazing heat without a single drop of water, and cats—another desert creature—historically needed their own mechanism to deal with water scarcity as well.

Unlike camels, cats do not have the ability to consume an exceptional amount of water when it is available and store it in their bodies for later use, and they aren't particularly well adapted to withstand dehydration either. The adaptation that allows them to live in arid regions is simply to be more efficient than most animals are with the limited water they have. After filtering waste materials from the blood, their kidneys reabsorb an unusual amount of liquid, recycling as much fluid back into the bloodstream as possible and sacrificing the absolute minimum to make urine.

As a devotee of both beer and coffee, a pattern of rapid alternation between drinking and urinating is pretty much a way of life for me. To a somewhat lesser extent, this is the same pattern that most non-desert animals follow: when water is readily accessible, pissing away large amounts of it fairly often is no big deal. It can always be replaced by drinking more. So most animals drink a lot and urinate a lot, ridding their bodies of waste materials relatively frequently and never giving them a chance to accumulate to the point of doing them any harm.

If normal animal urine can be envisioned as a thin broth of bacteria, minerals and miscellaneous crap that's been filtered from the bloodstream, then cat urine is—if you'll pardon the disgusting pun—like a thick pea soup. By the time they get around to eliminating waste material in the form of urine, they have concentrated toxins in their bladders to a fairly exceptional extent. For their ancestors, this was a valuable way to save water; these days, when obtaining water is not usually a problem, it tends to cause more difficulties than it solves.

People often make up fake disease names by adding "-itis" to the end of words, like "senioritis", for example (just as they make up fake addictions by adding "-aholic"). Never mind that, interpreted literally, such a disease would consist of the inflammation of one's senior (or that there is no such thing as "workahol"), we generally know what they mean.

When it comes to cats and their urinary tract diseases, though, this same kind of lazy labeling can sometimes be very confusing.

An actual urinary tract infection is just that: a bacterial infection of the urinary tract. Cats of either sex can develop infections periodically, although this tends not to be overly common and they can generally be cured quite easily with antibiotics. Vegetarian cats are no more susceptible to developing actual infections than anyone else. There is, however, another urinary tract condition from which a certain percentage of cats suffer chronically that *can* be exacerbated by a vegetarian diet. Many vets, choosing inexplicably to confuse the issue unnecessarily, will refer to this as a "urinary tract infection" as well. But that's simply not what it is.

This kind of so-called "urinary tract infection" is more correctly known as either FUS (feline urologic syndrome) or FLUTD (feline lower urinary tract disease).

Under certain circumstances, the minerals that cats concentrate in their urine can spontaneously arrange themselves into "crystals" (which, as their name implies, are actually quite beautiful under the microscope) while still inside the bladder. In females, this is not considered to be a major medical risk; the next time they're in the litter box, they'll simply pee the crystals out. The worst that can happen is that the urinary tract become irritated and causes discomfort. For males prone to FLUTD, however, there is the additional danger that if enough crystals form and aggregate, the urethra can actually become blocked. There is an obvious anatomical reason why this can't happen to females.

The symptoms of a cat suffering from either a real infection or a fake, so-called "infection" are similar; they may squat longer and more frequently in the litter box than normal, void smaller than normal quantities of urine, urinate outside the litter box, and/or urinate blood. Social withdrawal (hiding, especially on a cold surface like tile or a cement basement floor), and loss of appetite are common additional symptoms. When you know what to look for, urinary tract problems are easy to recognize; and even when you don't, it is generally extremely obvious that something is wrong. That is fortunate because blockage is a very serious medical condition; the sooner a blocked cat can get to a vet, the better.

In the first edition of *Obligate Carnivore*, I spoke at length about Jude and his struggles with urinary tract problems. I quote myself:

> Fat cats, in general, are more likely to have chronic problems with urinary crystals than skinny ones, and it is my distinct impression (through completely unscientific observation) that a disproportionate

number of orange cats, for whatever reason, do as well. Throw in the extra challenge of vegetarianism and a fat little pumpkin like Jude just doesn't stand a chance. Sure enough, he became blocked.

Fortunately, I had noticed his symptoms almost immediately and brought him in to the vet before his bladder had become overly full. Once the crystal plug that was causing the obstruction was removed, he was again able to urinate normally without further treatment.

Naturally, despite a history of extreme patience and understanding about my unusual practice of feeding my cats a vegan diet, the doctor strongly recommended that I switch him to one of the "Prescription" diets to avoid a recurrence. Unwilling to compromise my ethics, I refused. Within a couple of weeks, he blocked again. And this time he was not so lucky.

By the time I realized what was wrong this time, his bladder had been distended for so long that, even once the blockage had been removed and it was emptied, normal functioning did not immediately return. To get him back to normal this time would require a much more extended course of treatment: he would need to take several drugs, and, in the few days while they were doing their work, he'd need a catheter to allow the urine to pass. Worst of all, to prevent him from pulling the catheter out, he'd need to remain in a hospital cage with one of those plastic cones on his head and his back legs tied together with gauze until he was better. Once again, the vets insisted that I put him on a "Prescription" diet, and this time I agreed, temporarily, until I had time to figure out what was in those diets that made them work and see if a vegan version were possible.

The "Prescription" diets, as it turned out, have three secrets:

First, they are very low in magnesium. Cats do have a nutritional need for magnesium, but it is very low, and whatever amount they take in above this required amount is excreted in their urine. There are several types of crystals but by far the most common is called struvite and is made from magnesium and ammonium phosphate combined with water. The less magnesium that is consumed, the logic goes, the less that will be available in the urine to make into crystals.

James Peden states that the average magnesium content of meat cat food is .16%, while the recipes made with his Vegecat supplement, when made with VegeYeast (specially formulated for cats) and tofu coagulated with nigariko (calcium sulfate) rather than nigari (magnesium chloride) range from .072 to .168.

In other words, the vegan foods are actually better, on average, than meat foods in this way. Even the "Prescription" diets are only as low as .06

or .07, in the same range as VegeKibble (the lowest in magnesium of the Vegecat recipes).

The second secret constituent of the "Prescription" diets is an abundance of the amino acid methionine, which acts as a urinary acidifier.

The normal pH range of cat urine is 6.0-6.5, and struvite crystals normally require a more alkaline environment (7.0 or higher) before they will form. Jude's pH was 8.5.

It is not entirely understood why some cats are more susceptible than others to crystals formation, but it is only somewhere in the range of 10-15% of cats who seem to develop them chronically, while the rest will experience them occasionally if at all. In other words, 85-90% of cats will have reasonably good urinary tract health no matter what they eat. 85-90% can eat Friskies without getting crystals. And 85-90% will be perfectly fine on a vegan diet, with no additional precautions necessary. But for the 10-15% for whom Friskies is not adequate, a vegan diet, without proper supplementation, can be a real challenge.

The difficulty in controlling urinary tract problems while on a vegan diet is quite simply the fact that animal protein (fish is an exception) tends to be more acidic than plant protein. A meat-based diet produces a urinary pH that is less favorable to the formation of struvite crystals than one based on soy or other vegetables. The vegan cat food manufacturers, of course, are well aware of this tendency and compensate by adding the same amino acid urinary acidifier used by the "Prescription" diets, methionine. This, for the 85-90% of cats who are not prone to developing urinary tract problems, is sufficient to maintain a healthy pH. Yet for the remaining 10-15%, Jude squarely among them, it is not.

There are, fortunately, a couple of things that can be done: some enzyme formulas are specially supplemented with methionine, vitamin C, and/or cranberry extract which can help both to keep the pH under control and soothe the urinary tract to minimize inflammation. These formulas are probably not strong enough to reverse a case like Jude's all by themselves, but they can be helpful in preventing symptoms in cats with more mild tendencies.

The next step up in terms of strength is a version of Vegecat that has been specially designed for cats with this problem: Vegecat pH. This is exactly the same as Vegecat, except with more acidifying power (i.e., additional methionine); in effect, it is the "Prescription" diet of the vegan cat food world! Depending on the severity of a cat's pH balancing difficulties, switching to Vegecat pH may or may not be sufficient to deal with the problem on its own.

For Jude, it was necessary to pull out the big guns; I had to get him methionine pills. Only in this way could I get his dosage up to the level the meat "Prescription" diets would supply and bring his pH all the way down to normal. What is interesting is that while many vets insist that switching to a "Prescription" diet is the only way to remedy a high pH, most of them actually have methionine pills sitting on their shelves and could easily prescribe you a dosage that would do the exact same thing. When they recommend the "Prescription" diets as the only solution, it is almost as if they are saying that the only way to cure a headache is to eat a cake that has aspirin inside, rather than just giving you the aspirin itself.

The final secret ingredient used by the "Prescription" diets is—are you ready for this?— salt.

"You really need to use one of the 'Prescription' diets," I was counseled after Jude blocked the second time. "It's really important that he gets sodium chloride right now."

Now I may have skipped a chemistry class or two in my day, but I'm no dummy. I know H_2O means water, and I vaguely recall that $NaCl$ thing meaning something too. "You mean... salt?" I asked.

"Yes."

"Then why can't I just salt his regular food?"

"Well... you can."

Salt does nothing in itself; it is simply a way of getting cats to want to drink more (same reason the pretzels at bars are complimentary), which makes them urinate more frequently, flushing out the bladder and giving the minerals contained within less time to crystalize. It's not a good idea to add too much salt on an ongoing basis, but this is something that can be done quite easily during the time immediately following a crisis. Better still are some other ways of getting cats to consume more water that can be done all of the time: many cats seem to prefer to drink running water, and using a special kitty drinking fountain instead of a regular old water bowl is often an easy way to increase their consumption. Finally, you don't need a doctorate and white lab coat to figure out that you can get more water into your cats' diet by simply adding water to their food, or giving them foods that have a higher moisture content.

Dry cat and dog food came to prominence during WWII, when metal became too precious to be wasted on canning the wet variety. Although cats living in our homes have become accustomed to drinking a certain amount of water, they still may not be getting enough if they eat mainly dry food. This means that minerals may sit in their bladders longer than they should, giving crystals a better opportunity to set up and cause problems. As it turns out, the largest correlation of all between which cats will develop crystals chronically and which are able to keep these tendencies under control has nothing to do with whether they eat animal or vegetable protein, how much methionine is added to their food, or whether they are given a "Prescription" diet or not; cats who eat nothing but dry kibble (vegetarian or otherwise) have substantially more urinary tract incidents than those who eat at least some canned/wet food as well.

When I switched Jude to a wet food and started giving him 500 mg methionine pills twice a day, his pH was immediately brought under control. When I brought him back for his recheck appointment a few weeks after he had recovered from his blockage, his pH was still a healthy 6.5 and there was no sign of crystals. By all rights, there should be no more to the story, and now I should be wrapping things up with the moral that with a little perseverance, even this problem can be overcome. And everyone lived happily ever after without ever having to murder and eat each other or suffer from urinary tract symptoms again. The end.

Unfortunately, there is an epilogue. By the time a year or so had passed, and he was still completely symptom-free, I eventually started to get a little lazy and complacent. If I forgot his pill here and there, I didn't worry about it. When that seemed not to affect him, I cut him down to one pill a day as a regular thing. Then I took him off them completely. A couple of weeks passed with no incident. Then he blocked again.

It is important to realize that for cats who are particularly prone to this kind of problem, it is a life-long chronic condition. Through preventive measures, I may be able to keep his symptoms at bay indefinitely, but I will never be able to remove his tendency. Jude is back on his pills twice a day now, and I will not be stupid enough to take him off ever again.

Ah, but unfortunately that wasn't the end of the story either...

After several years passed without further incident, I had occasion to drive across the country with my cats. Several times each day, I stopped at rest areas and let them out of their carriers so that they could have access to some water and a litterbox. This was obviously less than ideal for all of them, but the rest took it more or less in stride. Jude, however, was too nervous to leave his carrier. My destination was my sister Shana's place in North Carolina. Jude made it as far as Chattanooga before he finally couldn't hold it any longer, and let it all out in the parking lot of a Waffle House. His bladder never recovered.

What followed was an agonizing series of relapses and rerelapses, as Jude blocked several times consecutively.

One of the difficulties in dealing with urinary tract problems is the fact that the symptoms can sometimes enter into a negative feedback loop. Stress can cause pH to rise, which causes crystal formation (many times, urinary tract incidents occur immediately after something stressful has happened in the home—new baby, driving all the way across the country, etc.—for just this reason), which causes irritation and discomfort. Which is stressful. Which causes more crystals to form. Which is even more uncomfortable. Which is even MORE stressful. And so on. In general, once this loop is broken, it is a lot easier to maintain a healthy urinary tract than it is to restore it to health once it has already gone bad.

This is why I have always advocated using the "Prescription" diets during times of acute distress. Although it is usually possible to simulate the low magnesium, pH and salt content of these foods, I regret to have to acknowledge that they seem to possess a mysterious X factor that makes them work faster than anything else. Remember, the purpose of veganism is to alleviate suffering; so, when your cat is suffering, the "vegan" choice may be to do whatever you can to make him feel better as quickly as possible.

Not peeing all day as we drove across the country caused Jude's bladder to distend and, due to his history of urinary tract problems, he lacked the resilience that cats normally have to regain normal bladder tone. Although the "Prescription" foods were sufficient to treat his symptoms, any attempt to put him back on vegan food—or even just 25 or 50% vegan food—sent him right back into another negative feedback loop, ultimately resulting in crystal formation and another painful blockage.

Was it "vegan" of me to keep putting him through this? I felt like I was torturing him, and eventually had to make two very difficult decisions: first, I took the vet's advice and had Jude undergo a procedure known as a "P.O."—which is an abbreviation of some medical term, but which might as well stand for "penis off"—in which further blockage is prevented by surgically widening the opening through which urine passes; and second, I resigned myself to the fact that he needs to be given meat Prescription food—permanently.

* * *

A couple of years after *Obligate Carnivore* came out, I surprised a lot of people by changing the recommendation on the vegancats.com website. While I still urged people to give their dogs and female cats a completely vegan diet, I advised people to give their male cats *some* vegan food, but to continue giving them some meat as well.

Now, as I have said, I continue to feed two out of my own three male cats a diet that is completely free of meat, and I should be very careful to clarify that I never intended for this recommendation to apply to those whose male cats have done well on a meat-free diet for an extended period of time already. However, for males who have previously been eating only meat, it is my belief that it is actually more "vegan", paradoxically enough, to only cut down the amount of meat that they are eating rather than to cut it out completely.

Urinary tract disease, in particular, blockage, can be painful, scary, expensive and a miserable experience for your cat and, although most cats don't develop any such problems when they eat a vegan diet, it is sufficiently unpleasant for those that do that it is well worth taking the steps to prevent it from happening in the first place. If I had never attempted to make Jude a full vegan, I could have spared him a lot of discomfort and I probably would have been able to maintain him on a half-meat diet permanently, whereas now he is eating only meat. The more conservative step of simply cutting down the amount of meat I give him might have resulted in my purchasing less meat cat food over the long run, and would almost certainly have spared both Jude and me (I'm an animal too, you know) a lot of grief. Hence, it would have better allowed me to achieve my objective as a vegan.

When Jude went through his ordeal, I switched him back to meat, but I didn't freak out and switch the rest of my cats back as well. However, this is exactly what many people in this situation do. And, what's more, they often feel the need to justify their decision by going around telling anyone who will listen that vegan cat food "nearly killed" their cat—thus starting the kind of rumor previously discussed and scaring others away from even trying in the first place.

To suggest that people should only put their male cats on a half-vegan diet is not hypocrisy, selling out, or even a compromise; after having carefully considered all of the various factors, I am convinced that it is the method by which we can prevent the most animal suffering the most effectively. And, after all, isn't that the whole point?

Making the Switch

I hope, if you have not done so already, you are now ready to begin working on lessening or eliminating what is, for many vegans, your final major link to the slaughterhouse. The only thing that may now stand in your way is getting your cats and dogs to go along with the idea.

Before I say anything else, I just want to make one plea: *before you decide your cat doesn't like vegetarian food, at least let them try it. You may be surprised.*

I can't tell you how many people have told me that their cat is too old to ever change, but that they'll start their next cat off on vegetarian food. *How old is too old?* I always wonder. *How do you know without trying?* Whenever someone tries to use that excuse, I always ask the age of the cat. Sometimes it's fifteen. Sometimes ten. Sometimes five. But it has never once exceeded the age of one of the greatest success stories in vegan cat history: a little old lady cat named Amber who made a fuss-free switch to veganism at the age of nineteen and when last I heard of her, was still going strong at the age of twenty-three. *And you think your five-year-old is too old to handle the change?*

If I had to name one vegan cat food that is most likely to gain immediate acceptance, Evolution kibble definitely comes to mind first. I have been told probably dozens of times about cats literally tearing through the bags to get at it. But the fact is that each cat is an individual, and you can never predict what he or she will like or not like. Some can't stand the kibble, but immediately go for the Evolution canned. Some will even be picky between the two *flavors* of Evolution canned, even though, in point of fact, I think the only difference between them is that one has potato and the other, avocado[35]. Some love one or more of the recipes made with Vegecat and will have nothing to do with pre-pared food at all. I can't tell you what your particular cat will like, and you can't guess. The only thing you can do is try[36].

I have heard of people who struggled for months or even years trying to get their cats to accept one particular vegan food, only to find out that the cats *love* one of the oth-ers that they had never let them try before. Switching cats to a vegan diet can be difficult, but it can also be surprisingly easy. In any case, the path of least resistance is to let them

---

35 it is probably worth mentioning, since I've been asked about this many times, that avocado leaves, pits, and outer peel are all toxic to dogs and cats, but that the inner fruit—the same part that we eat—is actually quite good for them. This is why avocado shows up both on lists of toxic houseplants as well as on cat and dog food ingredients lists

36 incidentally, since my retirement from vegancats.com, they have introduced a new brand of vegan cat food, Ami, about which I know absolutely nothing. Perhaps you'll want to try that one as well

try a little bit of everything to find out which one they are going to have the easiest time accepting. Taking the time to figure this out will make the whole process a lot easier for all involved.

Even if a cat doesn't take to vegan food right away, it doesn't necessarily mean that the food is no good, or that if they couldn't be persuaded to give it a try that they might not end up liking it. In fact, categorical, immediate refusal is almost a *good* sign; it shows that they are rejecting it based on a preconceived bias rather than making a considered, educated decision on the matter after having given it an honest try. They are rejecting it out of hand because they perceive it to be *different*, not necessarily because it is *awful*.

James Peden speaks of a substance called "digest" (as good of a name as any for what is essentially fermented chicken entrails) that is routinely added to meat-based pet foods to increase "palatability". (Kind of like how tobacco companies add nicotine to improve "flavor.") Interestingly, according to Peden, although "digest" is pretty much just chicken guts, some batches are considered to have a "beefy" flavor, while others are more "turkeyish" or "fishy"; and it is the type of "digest" that goes into a given food—not what kind of meat it contains—that determines which flavor goes on the label. Undifferentiated rotten animal parts with the "beefy"-tasting fermented entrails, for example, might be labeled "Beef Stew", while the same crap with the "fishy"-tasting guts is called "Ocean Whitefish". Cats that have been fed meat based pet foods over long periods of time can, according to Peden, actually become addicted to "digest" and such an addiction, like any other, may take a lot of patience, perseverance and time to overcome. Even barring addiction, we all know how stubborn some cats can be.

Fortunately, there are a number of tricks that may make getting new food accepted a little easier, and trick number one isn't really much of a trick at all: *you have to be patient.* Make the switch gradually, according to your cat's own pace. The first day, add a tiny bit of vegan food to the food they are used to eating; and the next day, a little bit more (each time reducing their regular food by a corresponding amount, so that they begin to learn that to get their bellies as full as they are used to, they are going to have to give the new stuff a try). Don't worry if they eat around the vegan food for the first several days; even just having it in their bowl and smelling it while they are eating will help them begin to think of it as food.

Sometimes to switch them over entirely takes weeks, sometimes even longer. But don't rush them. Make sure that you continue to make progress (i.e., don't get to a point where you are actually *reducing* the amount of vegan food that you are giving them) but allow them to progress at their own pace. Remember the days when if someone offered you soy milk, you looked at them like they were expecting you to drink a cup of paint, whereas drinking the mammary secretions of cows seemed normal and distinctly less gross? That's about where you can expect your cat's head to be at for the first couple of days. The "what are you, fucking crazy?" look your cat may give you is no different than the one you probably gave to whoever it was that first offered you tofu. Then you eventually tried it, and it wasn't so bad. And then you had a little more. And now what are you? A bona fide soybean freak. And your cat will be too, eventually.

Along those same lines, I'll bet that when you first became vegetarian, you didn't launch right into tabouli and hummus and raw lasagna and whatever else those crazy vegans eat for your very first meal. More likely you found it easier to begin with non-meat versions of familiar foods, like burgers and hot dogs, and your cat will most likely appreciate the same kind of baby steps. As you begin to reduce the amount of meat you are giving them, you can help ease the transition by adding small amounts of vegan fake meats: deli slices, imitation bacon bits, vegan tuna substitute. You do not want to keep these things as an ongoing part of their diet, but the (more or less) familiar flavors may make a vegan diet seem more acceptable in the early days.

Many cats love yeast—nutritional, brewer's, or otherwise—and a good sprinkling all over a bowl of mixed vegan and meat kibbles may help make them more difficult to distinguish, or it may even increase palatability to the point that they don't care. Oil (Olive or hi-oleic safflower are recommended), can also be used in much the same way. It is also significantly more difficult to eat around canned or wet food that has been mashed into their regular meat canned food until the two are inseparable than it is to separate dry vegan kibbles from meat kibbles. Any of these tricks may help to encourage sampling of new foods by a cat who might otherwise be less willing.

One thing not to do, however, is to take the battle of wills to the point that you are not letting your cat eat *at all* unless they eat the vegan food. Paradoxically, it is especially important that fat cats not miss a meal. It is a good strategy to give them increasingly less food until they are hungry enough to give the vegan food a try, but just make sure never to reduce it to zero. Have faith, they'll come along eventually; there's no need to starve them in the meantime.

If you suspect that your cat may be at risk for urinary tract problems, I strongly recommend not waiting for blockage to occur before taking steps to prevent it. The precaution of making sure to use at least some canned or wet food along with kibble (or even cutting kibble out altogether) can be immensely helpful in heading off the problem before it even starts. Do not use acidifiers though, unless you have tested the pH and found a need for them; methionine pills in particular are potentially very powerful, and there is a danger of over-acidifying if the correct dosage (based on weight and starting pH) is not given. In the majority of cases, enzymes pH or Vegecat pH can safely be given to cats with no particular tendency towards high pH, but a very small percentage of cats can actually have the opposite tendency and there is a chance that this could send their pH too low. This may sound confusing, but a simple test at the vet can tell you where your cat stands, and the doctor can help you figure out what, if anything, needs to be done to bring the pH into line.

It is a very, very good idea to bring your male cats to the vet and have their pH checked within a couple of weeks of putting them on a vegan diet. If their pH is found to be over 6.5 (or, in extremely rare cases, below 6.0), or if crystals are found in the urine, you can easily make adjustments to address these issues and correct problems before they start. Again, 85-90% are not going to need any adjustments at all, and making sure that they are eating some wet food is the only precaution that you will need to take. Given these odds, it may seem like an unnecessary hassle and expense to bring your cats in and have them tested. But if you happen to catch a developing problem before it has been able to manifest itself and become something more serious, it will have been worth the trouble.

Some people have reported that their cats or dogs experienced episodes of vomiting or diarrhea immediately after switching to a vegan diet. In a small number of cases, it may be because of a food allergy (generally to wheat, corn or soy, any of which can be fairly easily avoided if it is identified as causing a problem), but the fact is that most of the time switching to a vegan diet actually *eliminates* food allergies. Many, many cats and dogs are allergic to meat byproducts, although most cases go undiagnosed. Most often, initial digestive difficulties have a much simpler cause: the cat or dog has simply not had enough time to get used to their new food.

Cats in particular can be very sensitive about changes in their diet, and will often have these problems any time their food is switched, even between different brands of meat-based foods. Some extremely sensitive cats will even vomit at first every time a new bag of the same brand is opened, and even the variations between batches is enough to set them off. In most cases, the solution is simply to *slow down*. I always recommend a gradual transition between foods, slowly adjusting the ratio of old to new food over the course of at least several days. Cats or dogs who vomit or have diarrhea may have simply been switched faster than their stomachs could handle; reintroducing their accustomed food and then proceeding to wean them off of it more gradually is often enough to prevent recurrence[37].

Another thing that can greatly help is the addition of an enzyme supplement. In nature, dogs would derive enzymes from plants, while cats would get them from the stomach contents of their prey. Among other functions in the body, enzymes aid in digestion, and a lack of enzymes can result in the digestive problems that I have described. Meat cat and dog foods contain no enzymes whatsoever; and even cooked vegan foods have no enzymes (they are quite fragile and easily destroyed by heat). Although your dog or cat may have adapted to the point of being able to digest whatever meat food they had previously been eating, it is not uncommon for a more complex vegetable-based diet to initially

---

[37] I can't even count the number of people who used to write to me to say that they tried vegetarian dog food and their dog suffered from terrible diarrhea until switched back. "Beige-ish bag, pink label?" I'd always ask, and I don't think I ever missed my guess. Although many dogs do fine on that brand (Nature's Recipe), for some reason it violently disagrees with a certain number of them as well. If this has been your experience, I strongly recommend trying again with a different brand. You are almost guaranteed to have better results

overwhelm their system. Without enzymes, they may find it impossible to digest. The simple solution: add enzymes.

There is no point in waiting for digestive problems to develop before thinking about using an enzyme supplement; adding one from the start will help smooth the transition, and even if it is not necessary to prevent vomiting or diarrhea, it will confer other health benefits. It is thought that if the body is forced to make its own digestive enzymes (i.e., if they are not provided through the diet) over time this will take a metabolic toll. Arthritis, for example, may occur earlier and/or more severely in animals that have not received a regular source of enzymes throughout life.

Cats are all individuals. It's impossible to know what foods they'll like until you've given them some, or what strategies will work in switching them over until you've tried. The important thing is to keep trying and never give up. There are thousands of vegan cats out there, and there is no reason why yours can't join their ranks. At first, your cat may try to convince you that by making them eat a vegan diet, you are torturing them, but don't you believe it. What you know, even if they don't, is that switching your cats and dogs to a vegan diet is one of the most effectively ways available to you to *prevent* animal suffering.

Resource

Vegancats.com (http://www.vegancats.com): the online shop for all of your vegan cat and dog needs. It is the only place you will ever need to go, which is why this section is labeled "Resource" instead of "Resources".

About the Author

Jed Gillen is an independent filmmaker in Los Angeles, California. From 1999 until 2005, he was the owner of vegancats.com.

Current contact information can be found at www.jedgillen.com.

CPSIA information can be obtained at www.ICGtesting.com
Printed in the USA
BVOW05s0912240216

437904BV00021B/154/P